Explorama's Amazon
A Journey Through The Rainforest Of Peru

James L. Castner

Feline Press
P.O. Box 357219
Gainesville, FL 32635

Explorama's Amazon
A Journey Through The Rainforest Of Peru

James L. Castner

Feline Press
P.O. Box 357219
Gainesville, FL   32635   USA

© 2000 by Feline Press, Inc.
First Printing in 2000
Printed in China

ISBN 0-9625150-5-1

Library of Congress
Catalog Card Number:
99-97052

Table Of Contents

Fig. 1-1   The rainforest as viewed from the river. Higher light intensity along the edge results in a profusion of growth and the "green wall" effect. Vistas such as this led early explorers to believe that tropical forests were impenetrable.

Chapter 1

Introduction

The words "Amazon jungle" evoke images of lush plant life growing in wild profusion, of colorful birds and strange animals, of head-shrinking natives subduing their victims with poison darts and early explorers hacking their way through dense undergrowth. From the observations and insights of naturalists such as Charles Darwin, Alfred Wallace, Alexander Von Humboldt, Richard Spruce, Henry Bates and the scientists who followed them, we have learned much about the Amazon rainforest and its creatures. Even today during the age of lap-top computers and Internet access, the mere mention of the Amazon continues to create sensations of the mysterious and the exotic.

A tropical rainforest by definition is located within 25 degrees north or south of the Equator and is characterized by high rainfall, high humidity, and high temperatures. The rainforest around Iquitos, Peru, is approximately 3 degrees south latitude and receives an average of 210 inches of rain per year. Daytime temperatures are usually in the mid to high 80's with humidity ranging between 80%-90%. Each year around June, a weather phenomenon called the "Frio de San Juan" (St. John cold-spell) occurs, lasting from several days to a week. Temperatures may dip to the low 60's, forcing the inhabitants of Iquitos to bundle up as if they were in the heart of a New England autumn rather than the heart of the Amazon jungle. This close to the equator, daylight hours last from approximately 6:00 AM to 6:00 PM, with little change throughout the year.

The mighty Amazon is the Earth's largest river, which along with its tributaries in the Amazon Basin, holds one-fifth of the planet's fresh water. Scientists still debate whether the Amazon or the Nile is the longest river, but based on available information as to its source in Peru, the Amazon travels 4,000 miles until reaching its mouth at Belém, Brazil. It is so wide at Belém that an island the size of Switzerland is encompassed by its delta. The distance from Iquitos to Belém, on the Atlantic Ocean, is approximately

2,300 miles. The water level of the Amazon may fluctuate as much as 30-40 feet seasonally. Near Iquitos, its depth ranges from about 50-90 feet and the width is 4-5 miles during high-water season. It is not uncommon to see large, ocean-going cargo vessels on the river at the port city of Iquitos.

Flying towards Iquitos, in the Upper Amazon of northeastern Peru, you pass over what appears to be an endless and unbroken expanse of green. This is but a small portion of the vast tropical forest which makes up the Amazon Basin. Although the majority of the Amazon forest is located in Brazil, substantial portions are found in Peru, Ecuador, Colombia, Venezuela, Guyana, Suriname, and French Guiana. In its entirety, the Amazon River Basin covers an area approximately equal to that of the continental United States.

Although the total amount of land on Earth presently covered by tropical forests is only 6%-7%, they may contain from 50%-75% of the planet's plant and animal species. The Amazon Basin alone may contain as much as one-third of all life on Earth! The variety of living organisms found in a particular area is called biodiversity.

There is a tremendous amount of interest in the biodiversity of the Amazon region. It seems that no matter what group of organisms are studied, there are more of them in this region than anywhere else in the world. For example, there are approximately 20,000 species of plants in the United States as compared to about 80,000 in the Amazon. There are some 250 species of fish in the Mississippi River Basin compared to over 2,000 in the Amazon River Basin. There are about 850 species of birds in North America and over 1,400 in tiny Ecuador alone. The list goes on and on, but no group surpasses the diversity of tropical insects. Entomologist Terry Erwin once collected over 1,500 species of beetles from a single tree! His research increased the world estimate of insects from two to thirty million. Although some scientists disagree with these numbers, there seems little doubt that several million species of tropical insects still re main to be described.

There is much speculation about why the tropics, and especially the Amazon, are so rich in their diversity of plant and animal species. Scientists have formulated several theories to explain this richness. One reason may be the mild seasonality and nearly constant availability of resources found in a tropical forest environment. Winters or extended cold periods do not limit the number of generations of organisms

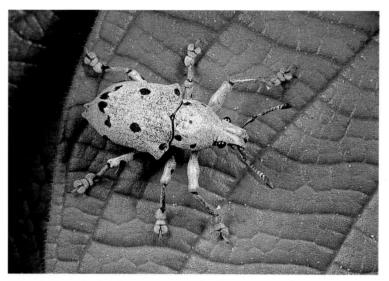

Fig. 1-3   An iridescent weevil. Insects are the most diverse organisms found in the tropical jungle.

Fig. 1-2   The heliconia is a tropical plant related to the banana and bird-of-paradise.

Fig. 1-4   The walking catfish or carachama.

per year. Evolution can continue unbroken and longer periods of evolution result in greater specialization of species. As Darwin's finches in the Galapagos illustrate, a finer partitioning of available resources through specialization permits more species to coexist in the same area. The rainforest's very complex three-dimensional environment offering more physical places where creatures can live is also a factor contributing to its large biodiversity.

Why is this biodiversity so important and why should we be concerned with its loss? The answer is because we literally do not know what we are missing. One-fourth of all modern medicines are derived from botanical origins from tropical forests. For example, chemicals extracted from the rosy periwinkle of Madagascar provided treatment that increased the survival rate of childhood leukemia from 20% to over 80%. The fruits, leaves, and sap of other species provide gums, resins, oils, and fibers for human use. Additionally, hundreds of species of tropical fruits and nuts have great potential for use in industrialized countries. Yet how many species have already been lost? How many potential medicines are gone forever because their plant source has been lost, as well as the human knowledge of how to use them?

The vastness of the Amazon rainforest suggests that it will last forever. This impression is especially strong when you view thousands of trees from the air as a solid mass of greenery. Even from the vantage point of the Canopy Walkway, trees appear to stretch endlessly to the horizon. This impression of "natural immortality" is however, a false one. Rainforests continue to be destroyed at criminal rates, along with all the diversity they contain. Statistics show that even today, less than 5% of all the tropical forests in the world are protected as reserves or part of a national park system.

Many factors contribute to the loss of rainforests. Most occur in poverty-stricken countries with few other natural resources available to generate income. Thus the lumber rights to vast tracts of land are sold off to industrialized nations. Cattle ranching throughout the tropics has also resulted in forests cut to create pastures. Sometimes even modern technological advances generally assumed to be beneficial have detrimental repercussions. For example, areas of forest in Brazil have been cleared to cultivate sugarcane used in gasohol production. Some lands covered by tropical forests are rich in minerals and petroleum. However, the extraction of these valuable commodities is often accomplished in a manner that scars the land, poisons the environment, and violates the rights of indigenous groups living there.

Fig 1-5   Ecotourism when conducted responsibly provides a means of sustainable use of the rainforest. Here bryophyte expert Dr. Stephen L. Timme of Pittsburg State University conducts a workshop on tropical botany for educators.

The influx of tourists to rainforest areas has led to the construction of new hotels, restaurants, souvenir shops, and increased employment in tourism-related businesses. Although the steady flow of tourist dollars helps local economies, tourists also have an obligation (moral, if not legal), to conduct themselves in a manner that conserves rather than damages the rainforest. Street vendors may offer to sell snake skins, animal skulls or necklaces with parrot feathers or even toucan beaks. To buy them only encourages the further hunting and exploitation of such creatures. If enough tourists fail to buy animal products and demonstrate a recognizable distaste for them, a form of consumer ecotourism will hopefully lead to the eventual elimination of such items from the market.

Ecotourism, indeed, seeks an alternative approach to the utilization of the rainforest. To be successful, it must have a minimal impact on the environment while at the same time show visitors the rainforest's biodiversity and its beauty. In order to be considered an ecotourism company, it is essential that tourist facilities minimally impact the surrounding forest, that alternative sources of income to local residents be provided, and that education about rainforest conservation be included for both local people and visitors. The protection of rainforest lands through the establishment of reserves should also be a priority for companies working there. Explorama Lodges has been involved in all of these practices since long before the term "ecotourism" became popular.

Fig. 1-6   Although many beautiful handicrafts are offered for trade, animal products such as the monkey and caiman skulls above, or bird beaks and feathers should be avoided.

Fig. 2-1   *The excursion boat Huitoto which was used to ferry tourists on day-trips from Iquitos down the Amazon River before the construction of the Explorama Lodge in 1964.   Inset (from left to right): Peter Jenson, Luís Carrion, Esteban Mosquera, and Antonio Montero.*

Chapter 2

History Of Explorama Tours

Many people have contributed over the years to make Explorama the success that it is today. However, Peter Jenson can be credited with the vision to conceive the idea and the determination and perseverance to devote his life to it. Whether greeting newly-arrived visitors at the airport, lecturing about the city of Iquitos on the bus ride to the hotel, or overseeing the transfer of groups at the boat dock, Peter Jenson remains the guiding force behind Explorama.

Born in 1936, Peter grew up in the state of Wisconsin. His appetite for the exotic began while he was still in high school working as a tour guide in Crystal Cave near Spring Valley, Wisconsin. His college years were spent at the University of Minnesota where he graduated with degrees in Anthropology and Geology. While a college student, he worked at the Minnesota Science Museum in St. Paul, Minnesota, where he later became Curator of Anthropology. As part of his work at the museum Peter appeared weekly on the *Bozo the Clown* show as "Scientific Pete of the Science Museum" presenting interesting specimens from the museum's collection. Peter has conducted archaeological work in the U.S. and on the Mayan culture in Guatemala and ethnological work in Mexico. In 1962, he began two years of research in the Peruvian Andes studying Provincial Inca sites with support from the National Science Foundation.

In June of 1964, Peter Jenson and fellow anthropologist Marjorie Smith met in Iquitos and started the company internationally known as Explorama Tours and incorporated in Peru as Exploraciones Amazónicas, S.A. In the beginning, excursions were offered aboard a 42-foot yacht named the *Huitoto*. Explorama Lodge was built in 1965 on a tributary of the Amazon called Yanamono in response to guests' interest in staying overnight in the rainforest. It consisted of only a single thatch-roofed hut with hammocks for sleeping and meals prepared outside over an open fire. By the next year, the facilities had increased to include a large house with eleven bedrooms and a lounge, as well as a separate kitchen and dining pavilion. Construction and renovations have continued through the years. Explorama Lodge now consists of eight separate buildings and has the capacity to accommodate 150 guests.

In 1977, a primitive facility called ExplorNapo Camp was established by Explorama along the Napo River for those visitors wishing to "rough it". The popularity of this idea with tourists led to the camp's relocation in 1983 to a more isolated location on the Sucusari, a tributary of the Napo River. The new location enjoyed nearly ten years as the most rustic of Explorama's lodges where guests slept in one large common room with mattresses, bedding and mosquito nets on split palm floors. In 1995, however, it underwent major renovations which increased both the amenities and the number of people that could stay there. Since then, the name has been shortened to ExplorNapo and a new facility called ExplorTambos has been opened in a more isolated area for guests still looking for a camping experience.

In 1985, Explorama Inn was opened for guests. Located 25 miles down river from Iquitos, the Inn is the only Explorama lodge located on the banks of the main Amazon rather than one of its tributaries. This facility made it possible to provide a rainforest experience for people who had only limited time in the Iquitos area. Separate cottages with electric lights, fans and en-suite, private bathrooms made the Inn the most posh of Explorama's lodges. With the addition of the Inn, Explorama provided accommodations to suit all tastes and offered programs in a variety of rainforest environments.

In 1999, initial construction on "Ceiba Tops - A Resort On The Amazon" was started adjacent to the facilities of Explorama Inn. Upon completion, it will contain 72 air-conditioned rooms and cottages with private bathrooms and hot water. In addition, there will be swimming pools and a hammock house overlooking the Amazon River. Telephone service and Internet access will also be available at Ceiba Tops, the first and only resort hotel directly on the Amazon River in Peru. The beautifully constructed site-adapted rooms are designed to blend in with the forested hillside they occupy. The unobtrusive nature of this resort is a tribute to its success.

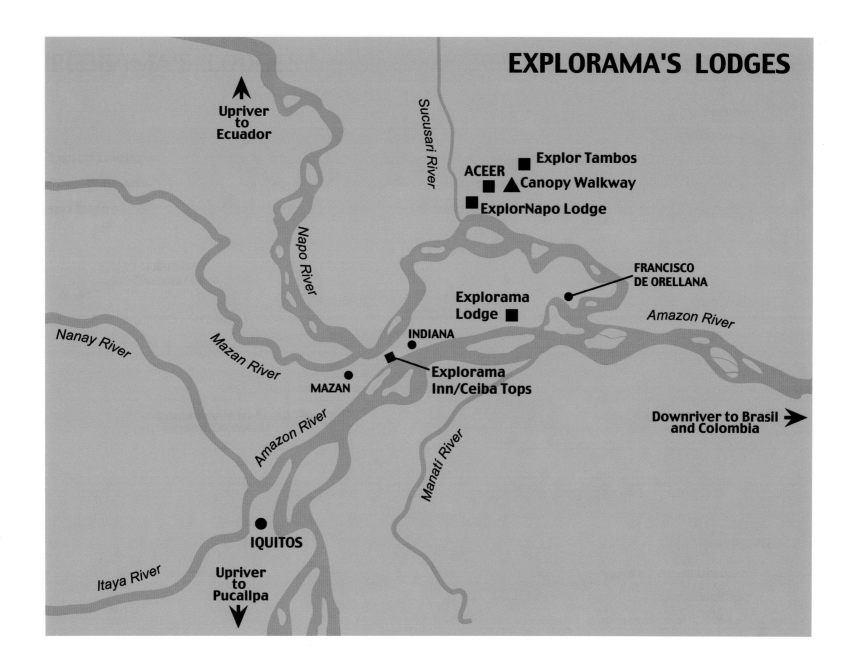

EXPLORAMA'S LODGES

Upriver
to
Ecuador

Sucusari River

Napo River

ACEER ■ ■ Explor Tambos
■ ▲ Canopy Walkway
■ ExplorNapo Lodge

FRANCISCO
DE ORELLANA

Amazon River

Explorama
Lodge ■

Nanay River

Mazan River

INDIANA

MAZAN

Explorama
Inn/Ceiba Tops

Amazon River

Downriver to Brasil
and Colombia

Manati River

IQUITOS

Itaya River

Upriver
to
Pucallpa

In 1991, Explorama hosted the first International Rainforest Workshop to actually be held in a rainforest, together with International Expeditions. This workshop, covered by CNN, provided the initial funding for the Amazon Canopy Walkway, an idea of International Expedition's owner, Richard Ryel, and a dream of Peter's since childhood.

Explorama Lodges has always used native building materials procured locally to produce lodges that are "authentic" and blend in with other structures in the area. A creative and competent staff of cooks prepare an excellent variety of meals. Chicken and fish obtained from local merchants are served as main dishes and complemented with regional side dishes. Menus include the bountiful tropical fruits available such as papaya, pineapple, and bananas, along with some less well known such as *cocona*, *aguaje*, *camu camu*, and *maracuyá*. Guests are surprised and delighted at the quality of the buffet-style meals served at the lodges.

Explorama Lodges currently employs over 100 individuals in positions ranging from boat drivers to tour guides. Many of Explorama's employees have worked in the company for over 20 years, and some like master carpenter Don Victor Sevillano, have been there since the very beginning. In addition to Peter, there are three other co-owners and mangers of Explorama. Like Peter, Pam Bucur Arévalo, Explorama's Reservations Manager, found the lure of the tropics difficult to resist. She first visited Explorama in 1985 as a teacher escorting students on a field extension course and later returned and stayed as lodge hostess for the next six years. Pam now lives in Iquitos with her husband, tour guide Aristides Arévalo.

Jaime Acevedo, Explorama's Public Relations Manager, was born and raised in Lima. After spending $2^1/_2$ years working in the United States, he returned to Peru and Iquitos where he owned and operated his own very popular restaurant before joining Explorama. Recently Jaime's teenage son, Jimmy, has become the company's webmaster as Explorama has jumped into the Internet age.

Luís Gonzales was born in a rural rainforest community and began working with Explorama as a guide. He later left to go to University where he received his degree in Business Administration. As Explorama's business manager, Luís now coordinates the workings of the company from the farthest lodges to the main office in Iquitos and handles all of Explorama's financial matters.

Fig. 2-3
Explorama's managers and owners:
(from left to right)
Luís Gonzales, Jaime Acevedo, Pam Bucur
Arévalo, and Peter Jenson.

Fig. 2-4
Explorama's Office Staff (standing from left to right):
   Maruja Cornejo (Reservations), Alex Enriquez (Reservations)
   Cesar Saboya (Operations), Viter Ocmin (Reception)
   Alfredo Perez (Operations), and Marisol Rivera (Reservations)

Explorama Guides (sitting from left to right):
   Armando Del Aguila, Renilo Vasquez, and Amner Ismodes

Explorama Lodges currently employs 18 native bilingual guides, most of whom have grown up in surrounding rainforest communities. Some like Lucio Pando, Segundo Inuma, Aristides Arévalo, and Roldan Hidalgo have been with Explorama for over 20 years. True rainforest experts, they are capable of sharing a unique perspective of their home. Not only have they grown up in the rainforest but they have also gained scientific knowledge and skills from the leading biologists and naturalists in the world.

Explorama has generously subsidized scientific research in all disciplines of tropical biology, often making research logistically and financially possible. The world's leading scientists such as Al Gentry, Ted Parker, Jim Duke, Steve Hilty, Gary Hartshorn, Charlie Hogue, and many, many others have all worked at or visited Explorama's reserves. During long-term studies of the flora and fauna in these reserves, the guides have apprenticed with visiting scientists and have gained a greater understanding of the biological processes going on around them. This is often a mutually productive relationship with the scientists gaining as much as the guides. The result has been a highly-trained staff capable of communicating diverse information to a cosmopolitan group of visitors. Guides are assigned to every group that visits Explorama's facilities and always accompany guests on their treks into the forest.

As of 1999, when Explorama celebrated its 35th anniversary, over 150,000 guests had visited its various lodges. Explorama's attention to detail has established a reputation for reliability that has resulted in the use of Explorama by tour agents the world over.

Fig. 2-5   Explorama Guides

Sitting (left to right):
   Raul Petit, Ary Arévalo, Cliver Riojas, and Lucio Pando

Standing (left to right):
   Luís Mayanchi, Segundo Inuma, Roldan Hidalgo,
   Paul Hoyos, and Orlando Guerra

Fig. 2-6   Explorama Guides

Sitting (left to right):
   Basilio Sahuarico, Willy Flores, and Percy Reyna

Standing (left to right):
   Ricardo Rengifo, Celso Hidalgo, and Julio Parano

Fig. 3-1   One of the most famous landmarks in the city of Iquitos is the Iron Building. Constructed during the peak of the rubber boom, the metal pieces were shipped from Paris and assembled on-site in Iquitos. The architect for the Iron Building is also famous for his design of the Eiffel Tower.

Chapter 3

Iquitos

Welcome To Iquitos

No matter where your journey originates, the jumping off place for your exploration of the Peruvian Amazon will be the port city of Iquitos. Most visitors fly in to Francisco Secada Vigneta International Airport located on the southern outskirts of the city. Today's logistics are a breeze compared to those of only a few years ago. There are many direct, non-stop flights from cities in the United States and Europe to Lima. There are several daily flights between Lima and Iquitos.

For international arrivals, passengers step off the plane into the humid tropical air and walk across the tarmac to Immigration. Entering the airport, new arrivals pass through a hallway adorned with Shipibo Indian textiles and handicrafts made by local artisans. Following the routine inspection and stamping of passports, suitcases and backpacks are retrieved with the help of many young airport workers who scurry about in an attempt to locate and identify each individual item and earn a small tip. Only authorized personnel are allowed in the Customs (Aduana) area of the airport to meet a plane. Once Customs officials examine luggage, you pass out of the airport building and are met by an Explorama guide who escorts you to an awaiting bus. Passengers arriving from Lima need not pass through Immigration nor Customs in Iquitos. They can pick up their luggage and go directly outside the airport where an Explorama guide awaits all reserved passengers.

The ride into town takes about half an hour using Explorama's rickety-appearing wooden bus that wheezes and snorts, but never seems to break down. Hot tropical air blows across your face from the open windows as your senses are bombarded with a variety of new stimuli. Strange smells of open cooking fires, countless barbecues, and various tropical odors immediately assail your nose. If you arrive on a

Saturday evening flight, it is nearly impossible to reach your hotel without hearing the pounding Latin beats of *merengues* and *cumbias* issuing from bars and dance halls at decibel levels guaranteed to cause hearing loss.

Traffic consists primarily of three-wheeled "mototaxis" with a bench seat for passengers behind the driver and a little roof-like canopy to guard against rain. These taxis will take you anywhere in the city for a nominal fare. To the uninitiated who have not yet had time to establish confidence in the driving abilities of the local inhabitants, it may seem that stopping and passing distances are judged with too fine a margin. However, traffic seems to flow in a constant, if chaotic, manner without major mishaps.

History Of The City

The city of Iquitos was founded in 1864. It is located on the west bank of the Amazon River, which although 2,300 miles from its mouth, is still wide enough and deep enough to be used by large cargo and cruise ships. Situated only three degrees south of the equator, Iquitos is capital of the large northeast jungle department of Loreto. (A Peruvian "department" is roughly equivalent to a U.S. state.) The city is accessible only by air and water. Its proximity to several other major water courses such as the Marañón, Ucayali, Nanay, and Napo Rivers have made it a commercial center and staging point for exploratory ventures for years. A trip down the Amazon River will bring visitors to the "Three Frontiers" area where Peru, Colombia (near the city of Leticia) and Brazil (near the city of Tabatinga) come together. From a small fishing village with less than a hundred inhabitants in the early 1800's, Iquitos today boasts nearly half a million citizens as well as traffic lights!

The city experienced two distinct periods of growth and development in its history. The first came as a result of the rubber boom during 1890-1920. The area around Iquitos is rich in wild rubber trees (*Hevea brasiliensis*) of the variety that produce the latex that was in highest demand at the turn of the century. During this period, indigenous peoples were enslaved and treated mercilessly by cruel rubber barons who used them to gather rubber latex from the wild trees that were scattered throughout the jungle. An excellent book covering this aspect of the rubber trade is *The Putumayo - The Devil's Paradise*.

Due to the abundance of rubber trees in the area, coupled with its strategic geographical location, Iquitos became a flourishing hub of commerce. It was a classic frontier "boom town", reflecting the presence of huge sums of rubber-produced money in its ornate and opulent architecture and the extravagant behavior of some of its citizens. More recently, from 1960-1980, Iquitos tripled in size as a result of petroleum exploration and extraction in the Peruvian Amazon. Remnants of both booms can still be seen in the city today which retains both a frontier and tropical flavor. Iquitos is the largest city in the Peruvian jungle, greatly surpassing Pucallpa as the next largest city.

Plaza De Armas

As in any Latin city or village, the main action in Iquitos occurs at or near the *Plaza de Armas*. Restaurants, bars, hotels, offices, shops, markets, and even a laundromat are all located within a few blocks of the *Plaza* which is the main town square. The increase in the number of tourists passing through the city has resulted in the construction and refurbishing of a number of hotels during the past decade that range from excellent to mediocre by Western standards. The five-star Hotel Dorado Plaza, opened in September of 1999, and located on the Plaza de Armas provides the opulence of any equivalent hotel in the capital city of Lima. The four-star Hotel Rio Grande, completed in 1998, is located on the Plaza 28 de Julio. Three-star hotels such as the Hotel Dorado, just half a block from the Plaza de Armas on *Jr. Napo* (*Jr. = Jirón* = street), are also available. Other hotels, such as the two-star Hotel Baltazar, are quite serviceable with only minor deficiencies which can be embellished into excellent stories by the time you reach home. Most hotels have air-conditioned rooms and some even have a pool.

One of the most famous landmarks in Iquitos is the Iron Building. It is found on the corner of *Jr. Próspero* and *Jr. Putumayo*, and facing on the *Plaza*. This building was designed by the creator of the Eiffel Tower, shipped in pieces from Paris during the rubber era, and assembled in place. The ground floor is currently used as business offices, while an up-scale restaurant occupies the second floor. Next to the Iron Building on *Jr. Próspero* is the *El Pollón* or the "Big Chicken" Restaurant. Rounding out the

Fig. 3-2   An old photograph of the city of Iquitos taken from the Plaza de Armas circa 1900 during the rubber boom. Note the locomotive in front of the buildings. Compare the scene with the same street and buildings of modern-day Iquitos in the photograph on the right.

Fig. 3-3   View looking in the direction of the Amazon from the Plaza de Armas across Jr. Próspero.   On the left corner is Ari's Burger, a common tourist hangout.   In the center is the El Pollón, and on the right corner is the famous Iron Building.   As in most of Latin America, the Plaza de Armas is the center of activity.

Fig. 3-5   *Beautiful glazed tiles still adorn some of the buildings in Iquitos.*

Fig. 3-4   *A street vendor sets up his wares near a hotel in the hopes of attracting customers.*

Fig. 3-6   *The ubiquitous three-wheeled mototaxi.*

block on the corner of *Jr. Napo* and *Jr. Próspero* is Ari's Burger. This open-air establishment with a name that sounds like it came out of "Happy Days" is a popular spot to relax or meet friends. At any given time the clientele is a mixture of local citizens, gringo tourists, and tropical biologists. Its claim to fame is the finest ice cream in Iquitos, which is served either as scoops (*bolas*) in a dish or on a cone (*barquillo*). (Flavors personally recommended are *aguaje*, *lúcuma*, and *coco*.)

The majority of shops can be found within a few blocks of the *Plaza*, especially along *Jr. Próspero*. Stores selling *artesanía* or local handicrafts are common, offering a variety of items from beautiful "blood wood" bowls to petrified piranhas. Street vendors also hawk goods on the sidewalks outside the hotels attempting to interest tourists in earrings, necklaces, and other distinctive items. One of the most popular night spots is a small park with electric lights and benches that overlooks the Amazon. The result of a recent city development project, it begins at the corner of *Jr. Napo* and the *Malecón*, continues north for several blocks, and is locally known as the "Boulevard". There are various bars and excellent restaurants along this strip, where you can enjoy a meal and drinks at either inside or outside tables. Activity usually continues to the wee hours of the morning on the weekends, encouraged by those establishments that offer dancing and live music.

There are two recent additions to the services available in Iquitos that travelers making an extended visit may find of particular use. The first is a laundromat located on *Jr. Putumayo* just around the corner from the Hotel Real. The second is a Cyber Café located on *Jr. Fitzcarrald* across from the Noa Noa Disco. Here Internet addicts can rent a computer for a nominal fee and log on to check their e-mail.

The Belen Market

If you have a night in the city, you may partake of a walking or bus tour of the city the following morning before embarking on your boat trip down the Amazon. A stroll down the streets of Iquitos reveals many points of interest. Some signs of its former opulence during the rubber trade days still exist. For example, the facades of certain buildings are adorned with beautiful glazed tiles (*azulejos*) that were imported from Italy and Portugal. Other buildings bear decorative ironwork from Spain.

Fig. 3-7   The tropical market of Belen in the city of Iquitos. Nowhere is the bounty of the rainforest more evident than in the variety of tropical fruits and food items found in the market. In this photo alone papayas, plantains, bananas, avocados, pineapples, chili peppers, manioc roots, and others are pictured.

Fig. 3-8   Carved wooden household implements and utensils show a fine degree of craftsmanship.

Fig. 3-9   Peacock bass is an Amazonian sport fish with a distinctive eyespot on the tail.

Fig. 3-10   Two young entrepeneurs market a great protein source and delicacy - - the edible palm grub or suri.

Fig. 3-11   Medicinal herbs in the form of stems, roots, bark, leaves, and flowers are sold in the Belen Market.

One of the most bustling and colorful areas of the city is the open-air Belen Market. This sprawling tropical flea market has seemingly any item imaginable from sandals made from old rubber tires to wash tubs filled with edible palm grubs. There are sections of the market with food, furniture, dry goods, medicines and cut flowers to mention a few. It is as if a department store were spread out at ground level with each area delineated by an individual vendor with their own cloth, table, or wooden cart full of goods.

Fresh tropical fruits and foodstuffs are in abundance and make up a major portion of the market. They occur in a myriad of colors, complete with exotic aromas and unfamiliar shapes. Even well-known items like cashews and Brazil nuts may leave a visitor confused when they are presented in their natural and unprocessed forms. At a single "booth" one may see papayas, bananas, plantains, mangos, avocados, manioc, passion fruit, chili peppers, palm hearts, palm fruits, pineapples, and many more. The incredible variety of fruits, many of which are unknown to visitors from the United States and Europe, demonstrates the impressive agricultural wealth that a tropical forest can provide. Only cultural bias and an unfamiliarity with new and different foods prevent developed nations from importing and using more tropical and exotic fruits.

In a different but equally prominent portion of Belen, vendors in medicinal plant stands present an array of herbs, flowers, roots, bark, leaves, and stems all arranged in neat little piles. It is easy to see why the rainforest is referred to as "nature's pharmacy". Some of the herbal remedies are raw ingredients in their natural botanical state. Others are sold as solutions in bottles like *siete raices* (seven roots). One of the most well known is *uña de gato* or cat's claw, which is currently exported by the ton from Peru worldwide. Local vendors promise results from its use for everything from AIDS to impotency. Although the efficacy of some of the plants for sale may be doubtful, the market trade in herbal ingredients at Belen is brisk.

Anglers will find the fish section of the market of special interest, although in the equatorial heat it does not take long for the smell to become overpowering. Peacock bass are displayed with the prominent eyespot on their tail easily visible. The walking catfish is another common species which looks like a primitive armored fish but has an unusually beautiful scale pattern. Another catfish that will become quite familiar to visitors is the *dorado* or golden catfish. This fish gets up to six feet long and can weigh up to 200 pounds. It has exquisite tasting meat and is served in a variety of ways at Explorama's lodges.

Belen - The Floating Community

Belen is also the name given to a floating community visible from the river walkway in Iquitos. It can be seen from the *Malecón* by facing the Amazon and looking south. It is a haphazard collection of shacks and cabins constructed of mostly castoff materials. When the Amazon's waters are low, it sits amidst a sea of green weeds. When the waters are high, it is transformed into a floating shanty town reached only by boat.

Amazon Museum

In the Governor's Mansion or *Prefectura* on the third block of the *Malecón Tarapaca* is a small cultural museum called the *Museo Amazónico*. This museum has a collection of statues of native Americans representing a variety of the tribes found in the Amazon Basin, as well as other cultural artifacts of interest.

Capybara Breeding Farm

Twenty-three kilometers outside of Iquitos along the road to Nauta is an experimental animal breeding facility that is evaluating the feasibility of raising certain species for meat. This venture is being funded by a private company called BIOAM (*Biodiversidad Amazónica*) with technical assistance from the Peruvian government. The farm is located on approximately 275 acres of land. The main animal under investigation is the capybara which can reach a weight of almost 200 pounds. It is the largest rodent in existence and looks for all the world like a sleepy, overgrown guinea pig with webbed feet. Additional meat-producing species being raised include the collared and white-lipped peccaries, pacas, and agoutis. There are also experiments being conducted into the production of snails.

Plaza de Armas of Iquitos

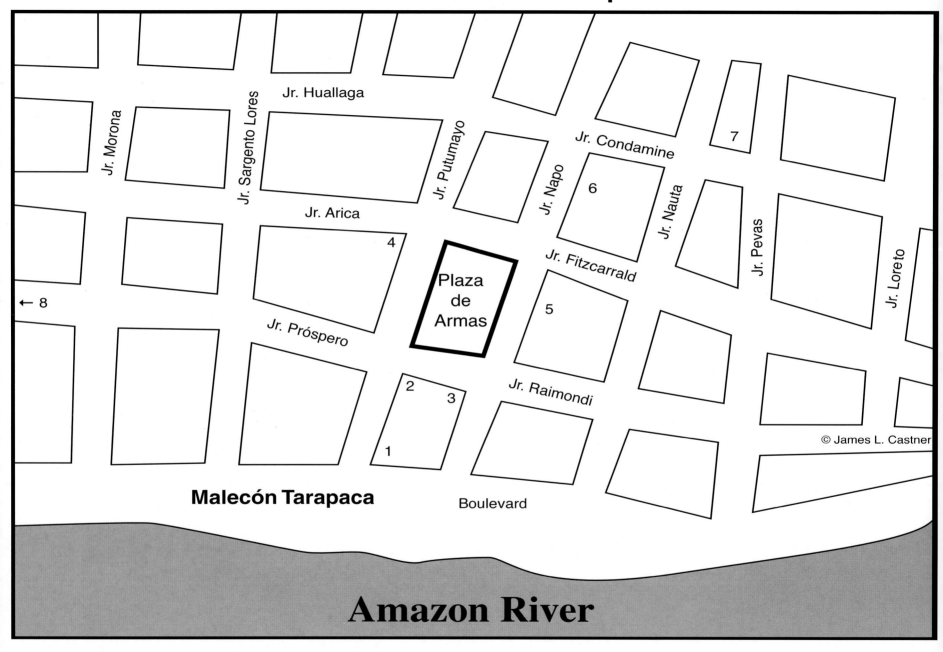

Jr. Huallaga

Jr. Morona

Jr. Sargento Lores

Jr. Putumayo

Jr. Condamine

7

Jr. Napo

6

Jr. Nauta

Jr. Arica

Jr. Pevas

Jr. Loreto

4

Plaza
de
Armas

Jr. Fitzcarrald

5

← 8

Jr. Próspero

2

3

Jr. Raimondi

1

© James L. Castner

Malecón Tarapaca

Boulevard

Amazon River

1) Hotel Real   2) Iron Building   3) Ari's Burger   4) Cathedral   5) Hotel Dorado Plaza   6) Hotel Dorado
7) Hotel Baltazar   8) To the Belén Market

Iquitos

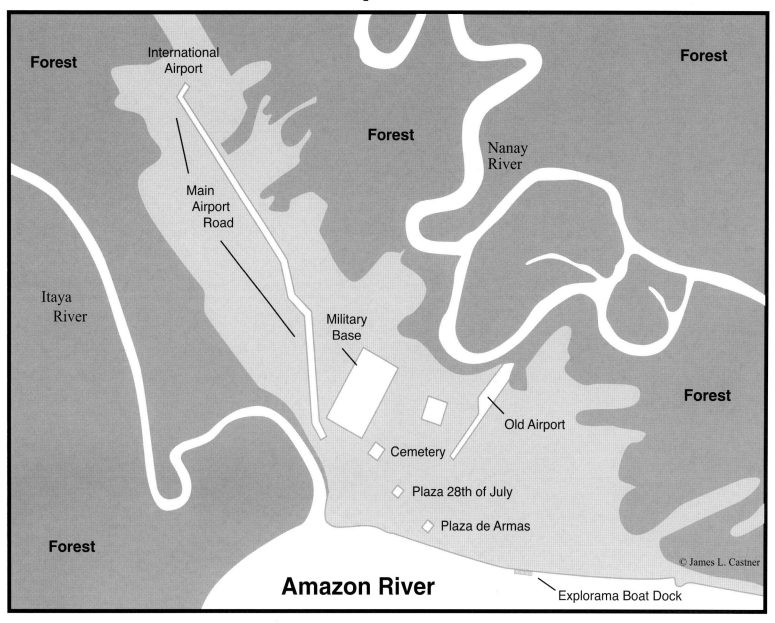

Forest

International
Airport

Forest

Forest

Nanay
River

Main
Airport
Road

Itaya
River

Military
Base

Old Airport

Forest

Cemetery

Plaza 28th of July

Plaza de Armas

Forest

© James L. Castner

Amazon River

Explorama Boat Dock

Fig. 4-1   A typical ribereño family standing at their homestead along the banks of the Amazon River with a backdrop of banana trees and tropical foliage.

Chapter 4

Life Along The Amazon

A short ride through Iquitos brings you to the orange and white building that houses the dockside offices of Explorama. A long set of wooden steps leads down to the floating dock where the fleet of Explorama boats is moored in the muddy brown water of the legendary Amazon River.

The exotic images so recently witnessed in the city are displaced by the scenery and vistas of river life. Leaving Iquitos, immediately on the left, is a lumber mill where sadly many of the larger rainforest trees will be processed. Huge trunks loaded on barges, their diameters sometimes greater than the height of a man, await their fate on the water. Further downriver, the petroleum processing installation of Petroperu stands out with its huge round storage tanks. As water levels change during the year, muddy sections of the bank cascade down into the water unpredictably. Reminiscent of glacial ice falling into the sea, it is part of a continual process of erosion of land by the river. Once Iquitos is left behind, the scenery changes little.

Cruising downriver, the boat may periodically pass small islands of floating plants. Upon close inspection, beautiful purple blossoms reminiscent of hyacinth can be seen. These plants, in fact, are named after that flower and are called water hyacinths. They are true aquatics, although sometimes they can be found growing along shallow riverbanks when they wash ashore. The beauty of this flower is so impressive that specimens were brought to the United States some years ago for ornamental purposes. Unfortunately, some escaped or were dumped into natural waterways where they have grown uncontrolled, clogging lakes and canals. States in the southeastern United States now spend millions of dollars annually to remove them from these bodies of water. Due to this recurring problem, with both plants and insects, inspectors of the Animal and Plant Health Inspection Service (APHIS) are very strict in searching for live material in luggage from tropical destinations.

Travel And Transportation

There are two main ways to get from one place to another in the Amazon rainforest - - by foot or by boat. In rare cases for those who can afford it, float planes are also available. While on the Amazon and Napo Rivers, you can see a variety of water crafts. Explorama guests ride in the comfort of powerful motor launches called *rapidos* (due to their speed). These boats carry up to 20 passengers each and are powered by 230-horsepower inboard Volvo engines.

The most commonly seen boat by far in the Amazon Basin is the dugout canoe. Constructed by traditional means from a tree trunk, their occupancy can range anywhere from one to a dozen people and the family dog. Paddling a canoe is as much a part of life to Amazonian natives as driving or walking is to people from the industrialized world. Even very young children are extremely adept at handling a canoe and can be seen entirely on their own, going about their business along the river and its tributaries. Those with least seniority often fulfill the role of bailer on family outings, using a gourd or shallow bowl to constantly scoop out the water that invariably collects in the boat due to rain, leaks, or spillage. Many of the one- and two-man canoes have an extremely low draft and sometimes seem more akin to a surfboard than a boat. Although loads of fun, the inexperienced gringo tourist is warned ahead of time to think twice before taking expensive camera gear for their first solo paddle.

One step up from the dugout in the hierarchy of Amazonian water crafts is the *peke-peke*. This is a long narrow wooden canoe with a very characteristic motor on the back. The engine has a straight shaft about six feet long to which the propeller is attached. This arrangement allows the prop to be quickly elevated out of the water in case of obstructions like floating debris or submerged logs. The name *peke-peke* comes from the monotonous chugging sound of the motor.

Fig. 4-2   *The traditional dugout canoe is the most common water craft seen in the Amazon Basin.*

Fig. 4-3   *Large double-decker missionary boats can sometimes be seen along the rivers.*

Fig. 4-4   *A peke-peke is a narrow motorized canoe that has an engine with a long horizontal shaft.*

Fig. 4-5   *A river taxi or "colectivo" slowly transports people and goods from Iquitos to the outlying settlements.*

Fig. 4-6   One of the powerful "rapido" boats rushes along the Napo River with a group of Explorama guests.

The river taxi or *colectivo* is another ubiquitous sight along the Amazon. These bulky substantial vessels haul both goods and people up and down the rivers. Typically 30-40 feet long, a river taxi has enough room for 25-35 passengers as well as baggage, chickens, pigs, fish, bananas and other items and trade goods. A palm-thatch roof is the traditional covering, although you may see some roofs of galvanized metal as well. Travel from Iquitos to Explorama Lodge (approximately 50 miles) by *colectivo* costs a mere $2.50, however the trip would take slightly longer than by *rapido*. On the average, about seven hours longer!

A variety of other vessels ply the waters of the Amazon. These range from one piece metal speedboats to huge tankers, barges, and cargo ships that seem incongruous in a jungle setting so far from the ocean. Rounding out river traffic are missionary boats, large open motorized excursion boats, and gunboats of the Peruvian navy painted an ominous gray. The red and white flag of Peru is flown at the stern of all boats larger than a dugout canoe.

The *Ribereños*

The banks of the Amazon and its tributaries are dotted continuously with *chacras*, small landholdings of the subsistence farmers and fishermen that live along the river. You can clearly see the bounty reaped from the river and forest by river families at the Belen market in Iquitos. Only the temporary islands that are submerged part of the year are without permanent habitations. The soil on these islands does not go to waste, as many are planted with crops in the newly deposited silt left as the water level drops.

The people living along the rivers are known as "*ribereños*" which is a generic term applied to the people who inhabit the river systems in northeast Peru. It does not denote any particular ethnic background, nor is it the name of an Indian tribe. The ancestry of the *ribereños* is a mixture of Spanish, Indian, African, and representatives of other ethnic groups who have settled in the Upper Amazon. This varied genetic heritage manifests itself in skin colors that range from white to cinnamon to black, and in facial features that range from Native American and European to African and Mongolian. Their thread of continuity is in shared lifestyle and geography, rather than in shared ancestry.

Fig. 4-7   A group of ribereño children at the village of Manatí.

During hours of travel on the river, you can see dozens of *ribereño* settlements. Some are large thriving villages that even merit mention on a map, like the town of Indiana near Explorama Inn. Others are only a handful of families and huts that barely constitute being called a community and are too small to warrant their own school. Most villages however lie somewhere in between with 50-100 people inhabiting a couple of dozen raised houses. Two additional integral features of communities are a long low school-house (usually painted blue) and a soccer field with makeshift goal posts. The predominant religion practiced is Catholicism and families dress in Western-style clothing. The role of the women in *ribereño* society is to wash, cook, bear children, and help in the fields. The role of the men is to farm and fish. Dietary protein is provided mainly by fish, a commodity more readily obtained when water levels are low. Fish may be supplemented by meat in various forms, when it is available.

Tropical Agriculture

The *ribereños* are cultivators that live by subsistence farming, feeding themselves with what they can catch and grow. When there is an excess of any particular commodity, it is taken to Iquitos for sale at the market. The type of agriculture practiced by the *ribereños* is a combination of destructive "slash and burn" agriculture and the non-destructive use of the floodplain of the Amazon River system, where silt-filled waters renew soil fertility annually by depositing sediments.

There is no doubt that the *ribereños* cultivate and harvest a wide variety of plant products. You need only look at one of the *chacras* or local homesteads along the river to be convinced. It is not uncommon to see 10-12 edible commodities growing at any one time. However, there are several basic crops grown as staples, not only in Amazonia but in tropical countries throughout the world. These are manioc, rice, and bananas/plantains.

Manioc is a plant that goes by several names which include yuca, cassava, and tapioca. It grows as a bush about 4-8 feet high and has a straight, slender stem. The distinctive leaves are palmate with long finger-like lobes. The edible part of the plant is the underground roots which are covered with a brown fibrous coating. Often growing together in a clump, they look like large brown sweet potatoes.

Manioc is almost pure starch and accounts for more than 10% of the caloric intake in Latin America, as well as a staple food for more than half a billion people worldwide. It is easily cultivated by planting foot-long sections of the stem in the ground and letting them grow. The large storage roots that are eaten take about 18 months to mature, but can be left in the ground much longer as a low-maintenance storage method and then used when needed. There are many varieties of manioc, all of which contain poisonous compounds (cyanide) to varying degrees. The processing and preparation of the roots effectively eliminates the cyanic compounds.

Manioc is served in a number of different ways, the simplest of which is to boil and peel it like a potato. It can also be baked, roasted, and toasted, or ground into a soggy pulp that is allowed to dry into a flour. This flour is then roasted to produce *fariña*, a grainy meal that can be easily stored for long periods. *Fariña* can be eaten raw or added to almost any other dish. Manioc is also the primary ingredient in the fermented beverage *masato,* which is consumed by *ribereños* and Native Americans in the Amazon, especially during festivals. When preparing *masato*, manioc roots are peeled, boiled, and mashed by women of the household or village who then chew the manioc mixture and spit it back into a big pot or vessel. Enzymes in the saliva initiate and speed fermentation. The *masato* is ready for consumption in about 1-3 days.

Rice is another very common crop in northwest Amazonia. The *ribereños* make use of newly deposited soil, planting and harvesting their crop during the low-water season. The variety of rice most commonly cultivated matures in approximately four months which allows enough time before the rivers again flood the areas where it is grown. Early in the season, the leaves will appear a light green and look like what rice is, a tall grass. The grains will also be green when they first appear, but turn a golden brown when mature. Vast areas of the floodplain along the Napo river turn yellow-brown when the rice is ready to be harvested. In small landholdings, the farmer may use a homemade wooden knife to cut the seed stalks individually, while on large farms many workers with sickles are employed.

One of the easiest plants for a first-time visitor to the tropics to recognize is the banana. Almost every small riverside farm will have many of these tropical tree-like plants. Hundreds of varieties exist,

41

Fig. 4-9   The edible part of manioc is the starchy root, which is peeled and prepared in a variety of ways.

Fig. 4-8   Manioc is a staple crop, not only in Latin America, but throughout the tropics.

Fig. 4-10   The grated manioc is sometimes roasted in a large pan called a blandona to make fariña.

Fig. 4-11   Bananas (shown above) and plantains are eaten daily and are important commercial crops.

Fig. 4-12   Papaya does well in the tropics, sometimes forming a tree thirty feet high.

43

Fig. 4-13   Rice plants blanket the riverbanks along the Amazon and Napo during low water season.

Fig. 4-14   The "aguaje" or scaly fruit of the Mauritius palm is eaten fresh, made into jam, or used for flavoring.

Fig. 4-15   Cocona is a common rainforest fruit that belongs to the tomato family and is used as a breakfast juice.

Fig. 4-16   A ribereño farm showing manioc and bananas (foreground), Mauritius palm (rear right) and a mango tree (rear left).

from ones that produce small yellow finger-size bananas to others that yield foot-long red ones. Banana plants take 9-12 months to develop their fruit which grow on a long hanging stalk. Young plants grow from the base of the mature ones (suckering) which are cut down at the time of harvest. Although once classified as different species, bananas and plantains are now usually considered to be only different cultivars. They are native to Asia, but are now grown throughout the tropics.

Plantains and bananas provide a high amount of carbohydrates, calories, and vitamins in the tropics. Ripened bananas are sweet and soft, and are eaten fresh while plantains are usually larger, contain more starch and are normally prepared by frying or boiling. Even the leaves of the trees are useful, often used to wrap food. It is a common sight to see bananas or plantains stacked along the riverbank awaiting transport, or stacked high in a boat or canoe on their way to Iquitos. Banana cultivation makes up a significant portion of agriculture for *ribereños* as they are consumed in almost every meal and sold in all of the city markets.

Many other tropical fruits, nuts, spices, and crops are harvested in the rainforest. Corn and beans are also widely cultivated and easy to recognize. Papaya trees with their star-shaped leaves are loaded with fruit and easily overtop the banana plants. Cashews, mangos, and avocados are just a few of the items found in your grocery store that originate in the tropics. At Explorama's lodges, breakfast drinks and jams are made from a variety of native fruits and forest products such as *camu-camu*, *aguaje*, *cocona*, and *maracuyá* (passion fruit).

Education

Children are an ever present feature of almost any *ribereño* scene whether in the form of a nursing baby, adorable dark-eyed toddlers, or young kids giggling and laughing at the approach of khaki-clad visitors. You may be surprised to find that even on the Amazon, children attend school. Education is mandatory, although unenforced, through the sixth grade. In rural areas, schools are in session from April to December with a three-month summer vacation during January, February and March. Children attend classes from early in the morning until lunch-time when they return home to help their parents.

Fig. 4-17   Most Amazonian schoolhouses consist of one or two rooms in a building located next to the community soccer field.

Fig. 4-18   The classroom conditions in the Amazon remind one of the once traditional one-room schoolhouses in rural areas of the United States.

Schools are built and established throughout the geographical Department of Loreto according to the size of each community. They are usually low, rectangular, open-air buildings traditionally painted blue. They are typically the only structure in a village built on a cement slab and not constructed entirely of native materials. The one-room or two-room interior has a blackboard, a cabinet for school supplies and combination desk/chair seats for 2-3 students each. Although primitive by the standards of most visiting tourists, it also creates a quaint charm and calls to mind the image of one-room schoolhouses where a single teacher was responsible for the instruction of an entire community's children. Teachers in the rural regions surrounding Explorama's lodges receive their training in Iquitos. Teachers live in the village where they teach as commuting from Iquitos is out of the question. The villagers provide a house in which the teacher can live as well as food since the instructor does not have time to fish or farm during the day.

Adopt-A School Program

Many of Explorama's visitors are educators who have come to the Amazon to increase their own knowledge and enhance their teaching abilities based on experience. Few are left unmoved by a visit to a local school where they witness happy, enthusiastic children being taught with an absolute minimum of supplies and equipment. In order to provide a way for educators and other visitors to help provide school supplies, even after they've returned home, an Adopt-A-School Program was created by Explorama in 1994. Most recently the program provided more than 3,000 rural schoolchildren and 125 teachers with all of their school supplies for the year including the very important soccer and volley balls for recreation. More information about how to become a part of this project is available at <www.amazon-travel.com> or at any of Explorama's lodges.

Indigenous Peoples of the River and Forest

No one knows for sure how many Indian tribes once existed or have been wiped out in the vast tropical lowlands of northern South America. It is estimated that when exploration of the Amazon Basin began in the sixteenth century, there were some six million Amerindians inhabiting the area. Disease, slavery, warfare, and habitat loss have decimated this number leaving less than a quarter of a million today. By far, the greatest number of tribes exist in the humid forests of Brazil which cover the largest area. However, several specific groups are known from the Upper Amazon region.

The *Yagua* Indians are an indigenous tribe native to the Iquitos area. A *Yagua* community, with their own landholding, exists adjacent to Explorama Lodge. Although now acculturated, visitors to the village can see exhibitions that allow a glimpse into their past and culture, including their traditional ancestral dress and the use of the blowgun. In the area farther north near the Putumayo River along Peru's border with Colombia, are the *Bora* and *Huitoto* Indians. To the east of Iquitos in the "Three Frontiers" region of Peru-Colombia-Brazil exist the *Ticuna* Indians. The *Shipibo-Conibo* tribes are found in settlements along the Ucayali River in the central jungle regions of Peru. The *Shipibos* are world famous for their pottery and textiles which bear a distinctive geometric patterning. These linear designs are derived from those used by their ancestors in body decoration. Access to the city of Pucallpa has permitted the *Shipibo-Conibo* to export their goods worldwide. Finally, in the eastern border region of Ecuador with Peru are the infamous *Jívaro*. This Amerindian group, which prefers to be called the *Shuar*, is the famed head-hunting tribe of the Amazon. In a macabre and fascinating process, the heads of slain enemies were removed, skinned and shrunk to a size one-fourth that of the original. Today's laws prohibit the sale and trade (and making) of these shrunken heads or *tsantsas*, although a black market still exists.

Fig. 4-19   Traditional ribereño homesteads consist of a one- or two-room structure with a thatched roof, raised on stilts to accommodate the seasonal rising waters of the river.

Amazon Art, Architecture, and Artifacts

Shelter

The houses or *casas* visible from the river all have a characteristic look about them because they are constructed in identical fashion from materials provided by the forest. The traditional thatch roof comes from a palm called *irapay* which grows in the forests along the Río Napo, its tributaries and other areas. The long, slender lobes of the leaves are deftly woven together with the stem serving as a means of attachment to a support brace. Leaves are fastened along the entire six-foot length of each section and are about two feet wide when finished. Called a *crisneja*, it is the basic unit of Amazonian roof thatch. Laid down in overlapping layers in much the same way as shingles, *crisnejas* are then fastened with vines to long poles that serve as rafters. A new thatch roof is watertight and can last 5-7 years before being replaced. Floors are equally if not more durable and made from the outer bark of *pona* palms, which are easily recognized due to their large stilt roots.

Houses are intentionally built close to the river. This minimizes both time and labor spent hauling water, washing clothes, or carrying produce and goods to the boat and back. However, such proximity to the river requires that the owners take into consideration the seasonally fluctuating water levels. All houses are elevated on stilts, as are most of the Explorama facilities. During high-water season, water passes below the houses, and canoes are tied up at the doorway rather than the riverbank. All homes are open-air and unscreened, with only one or two rooms. Many are without walls entirely, while others have only half-walls. Cooking is usually done on a metal grate in a small attached kitchen. Most *ribereños* sleep on a mat on the floorboards beneath a mosquito net. No home would be complete without a hammock, which may be woven of palm fiber or purchased in the city and made of cotton.

Utilitarian Items

Various utilitarian objects are almost always present on a *ribereño* homestead. Canoes are essential and ubiquitous, constructed in dugout fashion. Paddles are sculpted with a machete from a single large

Fig. 4-20   Spars and beams of a house are lashed together using vines and the roots of philodendron plants.

Fig. 4-21   Roof thatch is made from the leaves of the irapay palm which are woven tightly together.

Fig. 4-22   Six-foot sections of woven palm leaves called crisnejas are overlapped against rafters like shingles.

Fig. 4-23   Cooking is ususally done on a metal grate over an open fire nearby, or more commonly, in a kitchen attached to the house.

Fig. 4-25   *Ceramic bowls are fashioned using the coil method, utilizing stacked coils of clay.*

Fig. 4-24   *A ribereño woman uses a pilón and mazo to remove the outer husk from grains of rice.*

Fig. 4-26   *Wide flat planks of wood harvested from buttress roots serve as the raw material for paddles.*

buttress or plank root. Since each family usually grows their own rice, they are also responsible for harvesting and processing it. The chaff is separated from the grain in time-honored fashion by pounding the seeds. This monotonous and tiring task usually falls to the women and young children, who accomplish it with a large mortar and pestle called a *pilón* and *mazo*. The *pilón* is a work of art in itself, consisting of a free-standing, one-piece vertical bowl that looks like an industrial-size ash tray. The *mazo* is a heavy wooden club, thicker at each end. Rice grains are placed in the bowl-like receptacle of the *pilón* and repeatedly struck with the *mazo*. Periodically the material is scooped up by hand and poured back into the bowl, permitting the chaff to blow away. The club may be so well worn from use that it is absolutely smooth.

Other useful items of interest include a *blandona*, which looks like a small wooden canoe. This is used as a container for mashing manioc, a chore performed with a *mazo* of smaller proportions that looks like a mallet. Another variety of *blandona* is a large, rectangular pan of metal about six inches deep with wooden handles at each corner. This type is used for the roasting of manioc flour into *fariña*. It is suspended about 3-4 feet over a fire and for several hours the manioc is roasted while someone maintains vigil and constantly shifts and turns the material with a paddle so it doesn't burn.

Most indigenous forest culture groups also make baskets. Although some are smaller ornate baskets, the majority are largely functional rather than decorative pieces. They are commonly used for carrying manioc roots and stems, charcoal, and fruits gathered from the forest. Many baskets are made on the spot at the time needed using the materials at hand, which also accounts for their crude nature.

Bowls are made both from gourds and clay. Gourds from the calabash tree supply round green fruit, sometimes astoundingly large considering the size of the tree that bears them. They are cut in half, scraped free of pulp, dried and make excellent containers. Ceramic pieces are made from clay dug from riverbanks and mixed with ash for strength. The clay is rolled into coils and after a tight spiral forms the base, lengths of clay coils build up the walls of the vessel. A shell, seed, or piece of manioc fiber is used to smooth both the outside and inside. When complete, the piece is allowed to dry and then "fired" by placing it in an open fire and covering it with pieces of wood for several hours. This crude "kiln" hardens the clay and completes the process.

Weapons

The ingenuity of the Amazon native is perhaps nowhere more evident than in the construction of a blowgun and the accessories needed for its effective use. Known in Spanish as a *cervatana* or locally as a *pucuna*, the blowgun is a silent and deadly weapon that is still used by tropical forest peoples today. Most range from 7-10 feet long, with variations in their design and shape that act as a "tribal signature" to cultural anthropologists.

Only certain wood can be used to make a good blowgun and the first step is finding a *pucuna caspi* or blowgun tree. A growth character of this member of the nutmeg family is branches that generally emerge from the trunk at right angles. When one of sufficient length, girth, and straightness is located, it is harvested and taken back to the camp or homestead. The only industrial items used in the manufacture of a blowgun are a machete and knife. Before steel tools were available, tribesmen used implements made from materials such as bone and sometimes stone.

The long section of wood is first carefully cut in half and allowed to partially dry. Next, a channel is whittled out of the center of each piece. The two opposite sections are straightened and aligned by bending them over a fire. When the fit is flush, a tar-like resin is used to cement them together. The halves are further secured by tarring the flattened aerial roots of a philodendron plant and wrapping the entire length in an overlapping fashion. For maximum efficiency the bore must be absolutely smooth and free of obstructions or irregularities. To accomplish this, the craftsman reams the channel out with a series of long, dowel-like pieces of wood obtained from the bark of a *pona* palm (the same palm used for flooring). In a lengthy and repetitive process, sand is poured in the barrel as an abrasive during long periods of reaming. The result is an incredibly smooth and straight bore that rivals a rifle barrel. The mouthpiece is carved from wood of a tree related to the mulberry and, when finished, resembles a large spool. It too is attached and sealed with the tar-like resin.

With the main weapon complete, the missles or projectiles to be fired from it must be obtained. The darts commonly used by northwest Amerindians are split from the leaf stalks of a particular palm. These foot-long splinters of wood are carried in a quiver fashioned from heart of palm leaves and are sometimes kept together with *chambira* palm fiber. *Chambira* is also used to weave a small rounded bag that carries the fletching for the darts - - kapok. This fuzzy white material comes from the inside of the fruits of the silk-cotton tree where it normally functions in the aerial dispersal of the seeds. A tuft of it is applied several inches down the end of a dart, moistened, and quickly worked into a spindle shape with the lips. The dart is loaded into the mouthpiece of the blowgun and propelled with uncanny force and accuracy from a quick exhalation of breath. The point of the projectile is sharpened with piranha teeth kept ready for use and attached to the bag of kapok. Although penetration of the dart is assuredly painful, it is seldom fatal. Death is caused by curare, a jungle poison coated on the tips of the dart.

Fishing spears or lances continue to be used by *ribereños* and Amerindians alike although blowguns are becoming less common and have been replaced by modern weapons such as shotguns. The most common variety of spear in the Iquitos region is 6-7 feet long and topped with a point or barb. The traditional shaft material is the flower stalk of a large riverside grass called *caña brava*. With the floral portion removed, an extremely durable, lightweight, straight stem remains. The point may be permanent or detachable, connected by means of a thin rope or fiber to the shaft. Today's fishermen use metal points with one to several barbed prongs. Older fishing spear tips were made from split or chiseled bone, carved wood, and even stingray spines. Simple bows, using arrows with similar points, are also used by *ribereños*.

Arts and Crafts

Masks, carvings, baskets, featherwork, and other ornaments are made by Native Americans of the Amazon Basin. Unfortunately, until recently there has been little interest shown in Amazonian artifacts as art, except by a few gallery owners and collectors. Much of the problem is the organic nature of many pieces and their susceptibility to quick decomposition in a continuous hot and humid environment. Contemporary crafts or *artesanía*, are representative of the geographical area or tribe from which they originate. Some groups still use traditional techniques to produce modern wares. Many stores in Iquitos offer *artesanía* for sale, as does Explorama Lodge.

Fig. 4-27   A Yagua Indian holds his blowgun up to his mouth ready to "fire". These weapons are silent and accurate up to a distance of 80-90 feet in the windless tropical forest.

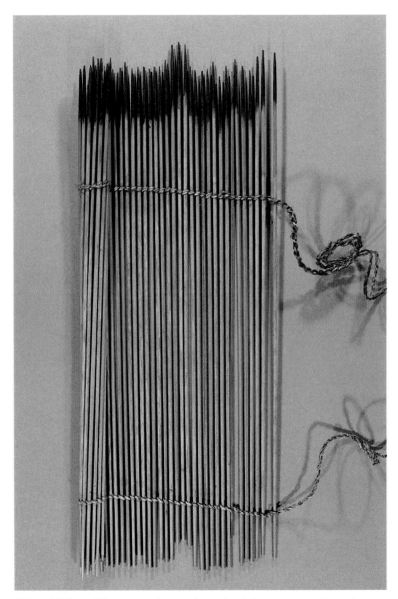

Fig. 4-28   Blowgun darts tipped with curare, a jungle poison made from toxic plants and/or poisonous frogs.

Fig. 4-29   Palm-leaf quiver and woven bag containing kapok, with piranha jaws attached for sharpening darts.

Ceramics produced by Native Americans like the *Yagua* in the Iquitos region are rather plain. The glazed polychrome vessels of the *Shipibo* are an exception. These fine pieces with distinctive geometric designs, although produced in the central rainforests of Peru, are available in Iquitos shops. The pots made by the *Shipibo* to serve as receptacles for *masato* range in size from small to huge. Some have effigies of human figures worked into their shape and design.

Chambira palm fiber is used in many ways, but especially for making large open-weave shoulder bags. They are often colored with wide bands of blue and purple obtained from natural vegetable dyes. Woven hammocks are also available exhibiting the same workmanship. Necklaces and bracelets combining fibers and seeds are also common. They occur in seemingly endless variations and make unique and inexpensive souvenirs. Beware of brightly-colored (red and black) seeds however, as they may be a poisonous variety.

An assortment of wood products are usually available, including roughly hewn animal and human figures. Bowls, platters, and cups made of blood wood (*palo de sangre*) are particularly attractive with their deep red grain. You may find the outer shell of a hollowed calabash fruit with exquisite carving of a native scene or animal. Half-size blowguns with quivers of darts are also available and usually made to represent the traditional technique. Although functional, their accuracy is not comparable to the "real thing" (they're for show, not foe!), and serve nicely to demonstrate construction methods and native plant use.

Body painting occurs throughout the Amazon Basin and may have religious, mythological, or practical significance. The two most common dyes are *achiote* and *huito*. *Achiote* comes from the seeds of the annatto bush (*Bixa orellana*). Also known as the lipstick plant, the bright red or yellow pods yield dozens of seeds that are covered with a thick red sticky material. Crushing these seeds produces a red-orange dye which is also used in cooking. The other common skin dye is *huito*, extracted from the immature fruits of the genipap tree (*Genipa americana*). When the juice of these fruits is applied to the skin, it soon turns blue-black in color, eventually fading after a couple of weeks. Remember this when deciding if you wish to experience a "jungle tattoo"!

Fig. 4-30   A woven bag and basket made from chambira palm fibers.

Fig. 4-31   Fiber and seed necklaces made at a ribereño community in the Iquitos area.

Fig. 4-32   A bag and hammock woven from the dyed fibers of the chambira palm.

Fig. 5-1   The newly constructed rooms of "Ceiba Tops - A Resort On The Amazon" blend in with the forested hillside landscape. The rooms are within a minute's walk of the banks of the Amazon.

Chapter 5

Explorama Inn
Ceiba Tops - A Resort on the Amazon

The 45-minute boat trip from Iquitos to Explorama Inn and Ceiba Tops goes by so quickly on the river that first-time visitors hardly have a chance to assimilate everything they've seen before the boat begins veering slowly towards the left bank. Explorama Inn and Ceiba Tops are located on a privately-owned and protected 250-acre reserve directly on the banks of the Amazon River. Its proximity to Iquitos (approximately 25 miles by river) makes it a popular destination for travelers who have limited time available to visit the Amazon rainforest. The superior amenities also make it an appropriate lodge for those who feel more at ease with the comforts of home.

Facilities

Explorama Inn currently consists of individual cottages sheltered by tropical foliage and arranged along walkways that radiate from the main building complex. Each screened cottage has a thatched roof, electric lights, fan, private bath and an outdoor porch. A generator that runs 24 hours a day supplies electricity to the cottages. "Ceiba Tops - A Resort on the Amazon", is located adjacent to Explorama Inn providing a luxury lodge directly on the banks of the Amazon River and within minutes of Iquitos. Ceiba Tops currently has 40 air-conditioned rooms with hot water, and even a computer room with Internet and e-mail access. These additions will make the Amazon experience possible for a wider variety of guests who have always dreamed of seeing the rainforest. Explorama Inn and Ceiba Tops also have a swimming pool, water slide and hydromassage.

Fig. 5-2   The tiled outdoor terrace of Explorama Inn is a favorite place for visitors to relax. Partially sheltered by a roof made of palm thatch, guests can comfortably enjoy birdwatching and other activities. The Toucan Bar is only a few steps away.

Adjacent to the Inn and Ceiba Tops boat landing, is a hammock house overlooking the Amazon River. The absence of walls provides a splendid view for relaxation at its best. It usually doesn't take long before the creak of hammock ropes can be heard.

A short walk from the hammock house is a beautiful outdoor tiled terrace complete with overhead fans, lounge chairs, and a palm thatch roof. The Toucan Bar, a spacious screened area where you can enjoy soda, beer, and mixed drinks, is nearby. For many, however, thirst is secondary to listening to the wonderful guitar music that emanates from the bar during early evening hours. As at all Explorama lodges, guitars are never far away and guests are invited to play and sing along with the musicians and guides. Beyond the Toucan Bar is the dining room where delicious meals are served buffet-style and an area where hot coffee, cocoa, or tea are always available. Overhead fans in both the Toucan Bar and dining room provide a breeze that may even entice a few guests to use a sweater in the tropical evening.

The Forest, Flora, and Fauna

Miles of trails extend in various directions from the Inn throughout the protected reserve of forest owned by Explorama. Main trails loop about the hills, intersected by several side trails that further penetrate the surrounding jungle. Many guests will spend much of their time hiking these trails, but are reminded to do so only in the company of their guide who is sure to point out things that even experienced rainforest travelers have never seen before.

The trails are rich with wildlife, but spectacular flora and fauna can also be seen near your room and along the cement and wooden walkways of the Inn. For those who are adept at observing quietly and have a practiced eye, nature presents endless possibilities. The variety of plants, birds, frogs, butterflies, and other insects is astounding. For example, interspersed among the cabins are plants with long banana-like leaves and pendent yellow and red blossoms. The flowers are actually small, pale yellow structures that emerge from the more colorful portions called bracts. These plants are heliconia, of which there are several hundred species in the tropics. Some produce long hanging inflorescences, while others grow upright from the forest floor. In both cases, the bright colors attract hummingbirds such as the long-tailed hermit, which keep their sweet reward and transport pollen in the process.

Another interesting tree called wild mango or anchovy pear is located on the lodge grounds. It is related to neither the mango nor the pear tree, but has fruit that bears some resemblance to both. The fruits are unusual because they are produced from flowers that are borne on the trunk itself. Flower stalks up to a foot long stick rigidly out from the trunk where red buds give rise to yellow flowers, followed by brown fruit. This phenomenon, called cauliflory, is repeated on many other tropical trees and plants, including the tree which provides us with chocolate.

Tank bromeliads with strap-like leaves arranged in a whorl or rosette can be seen attached to trees and are so named because of the water they hold in their leaf axils near the center. If you peer into the middle of the plant and the nooks and crannies formed by the closely overlapping leaves, you may see some creatures hiding there. Adult frogs use the areas around the leaf bases for cover, squeezing in as tightly as possible. Sometimes they are also found in the little pool in the center of the bromeliad. Mosquito larvae, tadpoles, and damselfly nymphs all make a home in the pool formed by a tank bromeliad. It is a self-contained miniature ecosystem, with herbivores, predators, scavengers, etc.

Other bromeliads found at the Inn grow directly from the ground like the pineapple plant they resemble. This type of terrestrial bromeliad also provides a home for multiple forms of life. Among these are the tiny dart-poison frog, especially *Dendrobates reticulatus*, a thumbnail-sized handsome orange and black specimen with a chain-like pattern of blue on its hind legs. The diurnal lifestyle and highly visible colors may seem contrary to survival, but this liliputian frog has a secret weapon. It is one of many species of brightly-colored frogs which if attacked, releases toxins from glands under the skin. It is this same poison that Amerindians in the Amazon Basin have used for centuries to coat the tips of their blowgun darts, hence giving the frogs their name of dart-poison or arrow-poison frogs. Their colors are a warning signal to would be attackers that says "Beware!" If an "uneducated" predator does attack the frog and try to eat it, the toxins will make it very sick or even kill it.

Fig. 5-4   A few bromeliads such as this relative of the pineapple plant are terrestrial and grow on the ground.

Fig. 5-3   Most bromeliads are epiphytic and grow using other trees and branches for support.

Fig. 5-5   Water collects in the leaf axils of bromeliads and serves as a pond for insects and tadpoles.

Fig. 5-6   *A common dart-poison frog in the tropical forests outside of Iquitos is Dendrobates reticulatus. These frogs often inhabit water that collects in tank bromeliads but can also be found on the forest floor.*

One of the pleasures of visiting Explorama's lodges is the ease with which many animals can be seen. For example, guests seated in the dining room of Explorama Inn have been treated on numerous occasions to the sight of pygmy marmosets and saddleback tamarins in nearby fruiting trees. Pygmy marmosets are shy, tiny primates only 4-6" as adults. They have tawny golden-gray fur and a tail that is almost twice the length of their body. These diminutive monkeys move very quietly through the forest, sometimes emitting a raspy chirp that sounds more like an insect or bird. Traveling in small groups, pygmy marmosets feed on tree sap as well as insects and certain fruits. They use their teeth to gouge holes in the bark of trees and large vines then return periodically to feed at the resin or sap that has collected at these holes.

Saddleback tamarins are almost twice as large as pygmy marmosets and are very different in color. They have a black head with a white muzzle, black feet, and a long dark furry tail. Their shoulders and fore- and hindquarters are reddish-brown, while the fur of their back is black with yellow or orange markings. These monkeys travel in groups of up to a dozen and are often found in densely foliated habitats with many lianas. Their diet consists of nectar, fruits, and insects, although they will sometimes feed on sap from the holes made by pygmy marmosets. Saddleback tamarins make several sounds ranging from soft trills to loud whistles. Explorama's guides are adept at recognizing these vocalizations and using them to locate their source. If approached stealthily, visitors may be rewarded with the sight of an entire troop engaging in spectacular jumps as they cross wide gaps in the foliage.

One of the most unusual mammals that may be seen at Explorama Inn is the silky anteater, also known as the pygmy anteater. Its furry body is only 8-10" long with a prehensile tail of the same length. Covered with golden shimmering fur that usually has a dark stripe down the back, it is seen less commonly due to its solitary, nocturnal arboreal habits. After darkness falls, the silky anteater leaves its roost to forage for ants, termites, and other insects amongst the vines and trees. The large claws of its front legs are used to rip open plant material and its sticky tongue licks up the ants found inside.

Since insects abound in the Amazon, where there may be literally millions of species, they are easily seen from all of Explorama's lodges. No matter where you are in the rainforest, whether you are aware of them or not, extraordinary insects will be close by. At Explorama Inn you may encounter the lanternfly, an unusual specimen attracted to lights at night and related to the cicadas that you see and hear so frequently during the summer in the United States. About four inches long, the lanternfly has a peanut-shaped structure at the front of its body with dark markings which imitate eyes and a row of teeth, giving the impression that this insect is actually a small but fierce looking lizard. This head-like appearance is actually just a strangely shaped hollow piece of the insect's skin and the real head exists immediately behind it. As for teeth, the lanternfly has a long slender beak which it uses to suck plant sap. Strange legends surround this insect which the natives call *chicharra machaca* (the cicada viper)! It is greatly feared by many local people who believe its bite is fatal. However, since the beak cannot possibly break human skin, accounts of the lanternfly's "bite" have been greatly exaggerated.

The wax-tailed hoppers, equally strange insects, are also related to cicadas. Often found in groups on the same species of tree, they are about two inches long, blue-gray in color and several species have red eyes. The bizarre feature of these insects is the long, white, waxy plumes that protrude from the tip of the abdomen and which may exceed the length of the body itself. These threads of wax are a natural by-product formed from the copious amounts of liquids and sap ingested by the insects. This may give it an unintentional survival advantage, because they are the most obvious and visible portion of the insect. If a predator spots the hopper and tries to grab it by the plumes, they break off and crumble to dust as the hopper flutters away.

Excursions

Bird Watching
Of the many people who visit the Amazon, undoubtedly a high percentage are bird watchers. Whether fanatical "life-listers" or more casual "take them as they come" types, the Amazon Basin offers

Fig. 5-7   *Macaws including the scarlet and the blue and gold are commonly seen at all of Explorama's lodges.*

Fig. 5-8   *A keel-billed toucan is one of many species of toucans and aracaris common along the Amazon.*
© Stephen R. Madigosky

Fig. 5-9   *The rufescent tiger heron is one of many water birds that can be seen on early morning boat excursions.*
© Stephen R. Madigosky

the highest bird diversity in the world. As one might expect, different species of birds are found inland as opposed to those found along the river, its tributaries, and the ephemeral islands that are formed by the river. Species composition also changes with the type of forest (flood plain vs. terra firme) and the level of the forest (canopy vs. forest floor). Expert training, a lifetime in the jungle, and unbelievably sharp eyes make Explorama's guides some of the best birders in the world for all of these areas. Every day before breakfast, they offer the opportunity to venture forth on foot or by boat at sunrise, one of the best times to look for birds. These early morning excursions are not usually long, as frequent stops are made to observe whatever wildlife is encountered, but are certainly some of the most productive.

Although many birds can be found at all of Explorama's lodges, one long-term feathered resident at the Inn is the great potoo. This large (20") relative of the nighthawks and nightjars is insectivorous and flies by night catching insects on the wing. Its brown and gray mottled plumage allows it to perfectly imitate the broken, stump-like branch of a tree. This disguise is further enhanced as the great potoo sits erect and motionless during the day atop a real tree stump or branch.

Some birds are as distinctive by sound as they are by sight. In fact, most world-class ornithologists can recognize their quarry by either eye or ear. The toucans, aracaris, and toucanets all have disproportionately large beaks, making their profile easily recognizable. The white-throated or Cuvier's Toucan also has a unique call. Whether you are sitting on your porch at the Inn or standing on a span of the Canopy Walkway, you will probably hear this bird's loud squawking which locals say is the repeated call for the toucan's "Tio Juan, Juan, Juan". The call of the pauraque, one of the nightjars, is another easy call to remember as it sounds like a wolf-whistle repeated throughout the night.

Yanayacu Lake

Accessible during the high water months from Explorama Inn, normally January to May, the blackwater Yanayacu Lake is fed by a blackwater stream of the same name. The term "blackwater" is misleading, as the waters of the stream and lake are actually clear, only darkly stained with the tannins of plant matter. These types of streams and rivers do not carry the soil and sediment particles such as are found in the whitewaters of the Amazon River.

Fig. 5-10   The giant Amazon water lily is often more than a yard across. They are part of the plant community at Lake Yanayacu. Here the lilies rest amongst water lettuce, while the large tree-like philodendron that is a prime foodplant of the hoatzin bird grows in the background.

Once the boat enters the serene waters of the lake, the motor is cut off and the guide takes over with a paddle. Slow, cautious paddling provides a close look at birds that frequent lakes and marshes. The wattled jacana, for instance, walks on the top of densely-packed aquatic plants such as water lettuce with its large, splay-toed feet. Other common lakeside visitors include the capped heron with its long head plumes and the rufescent tiger heron. The anhinga may also be seen, with just its sinuous neck and head visible as it slices through the water in search of fish. This behavior has also given it the name "snake-bird". With feathers that lack the ability to shed water, the anhinga must dry its wings by sunning them so it is not uncommon to see one sitting on a perch with wings spread in a perfect pose.

It requires a little more work to get a close look at one of the most famous and feared Amazon denizens that inhabit the lake - - the piranha. Lines, hooks, and bait are provided and the combined efforts of passengers and crew usually result in at least one of these fish. The ferocious nature of piranhas has been greatly exaggerated in movies and books. Most feed on small fish while some are even fruit-eaters, adapted to taking advantage of the bounty that falls in the rivers and flooded forest. Of the many species described, only four or five are potentially dangerous to man. These cut-and-slash predators, usually only 6-10 inches long, are armed with sharp triangular teeth. Although their normal prey is fish, they are sensitive to blood in the water. Actual accounts of hordes of ravenous fish attacking a human or animal though, are few. The most likely explanation for such behavior is that fish become trapped in a diminishing body of water where their natural food supply is exhausted. If starving, they will naturally attack anything.

A less threatening yet equally impressive example of the wildlife that inhabits Yanayacu Lake can be found floating on the water's surface near the lake's edges. The giant Amazon lily pad, still commonly called the Queen Victoria water lily, is technically the *Victoria amazonica*. These immense lily pads may sometimes measure more than a yard in diameter. Although less fearsome than a piranha, they too can draw blood. You should resist the urge to reach down and grab these plants, as the purple bottoms are covered with extremely large, sharp spines! Its flower opens only after sunset and is originally white. Beetles are attracted to its scent in the darkness, but become trapped inside when the blossom closes before dawn. They pass the day in their floral jail, picking up pollen, and carry it off on the following night when the now rose-colored flower opens once again.

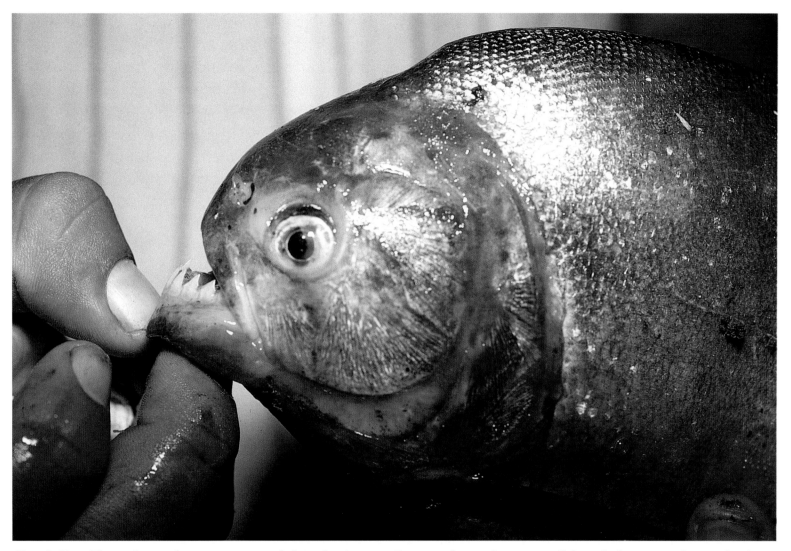

Fig. 5-11   The red piranha is a common fish in the Amazon River and its tributaries. Although the triangular teeth of this fish are razor sharp, they are seldom aggressive towards people or large animals.

The Giant Ceiba Tree

A sad legacy has been left the world as a result of the loggers that have passed through the north-west Amazon. Most of the towering rainforest giants have succumbed to the timber industry, especially those near rivers where they could be easily transported to mills. Among these species, highly prized for their wood and able to grow high enough to emerge through the canopy of the tropical forest, is the giant ceiba or kapok tree (*Ceiba pentandra*).

A short walk from the Inn and Ceiba Tops along the trail that leads to the village of Indiana, is a lone, mature ceiba tree that inspired the name of the new resort. Beginning at ground level, you see huge wall-like buttress roots that extend as high as 20-30 feet up the trunk. Historical accounts tell of enormous specimens whose roots covered almost an entire acre of ground. Continuing upward is a straight trunk of tremendous girth, yet completely devoid of branches until near the summit, where large branches produce a beautiful and distinctive crown. The profile of this particular tree is silhouetted against the sky and visible from boats traveling downriver from Explorama Inn and Ceiba Tops.

As you look at the branches of the ceiba tree, you will see that they are festooned with epiphytes. These plants are not parasites as they only use the branches for support, but take their nourishment from the rain, mist, and decomposing organic material that accumulates on the limbs. Many of these epiphytes are tank bromeliads, such as the ones seen at ground level near the Inn. As with terrestrial bromeliads, miniature ponds, each with their own fauna of insects and frogs, will occur a hundred feet above the ground when the bromeliads grow on emergent trees.

Kapok is not only a name of this tree, but also names a product which it produces and which had widespread commercial use decades ago. Hundreds of 8-10 inch long woody capsular fruits are produced on the tree periodically. Inside, they are stuffed with a cottony material known as "kapok". This material is released when the fruits split, floating to the forest floor on whatever wind currents are available, carrying the tree's seeds along with it. Due to the light quality of the kapok, it was used for many years as a stuffing in life preservers. Amerindians throughout the Amazon Basin have their own practical use for it. They carefully wad and shape it onto the rear portion of a dart before loading it into a blowgun where it fills the diameter of the bore or barrel of the weapon so that when the user blows, the air pushes the cotton wad out and the dart along with it.

Fig. 5-12   The new "Ceiba Tops" resort is named for the giant ceiba tree shown above. This tree is only a short walk to the east of the lodge. The towering branches of the tree's crown are covered with epiphytic bromeliads.

Indiana

One of the larger villages along the Amazon River, Indiana is a community of over 3,500 inhabitants. Prosperous by Amazonian standards, this town has running water in most of the houses and electricity for about six hours a day which even provides street lights. Indiana has a small hospital with a doctor and nurse, as well as Elementary, Secondary, Agricultural, and Occupational schools. Originally a Franciscan mission town, it remains a religious community with one Catholic and six Evangelical churches. Various scheduled river boats are available daily between Indiana and Iquitos.

Fig. 5-13   The village of Indiana on the Amazon River near Explorama Inn is prosperous by Amazonian standards. It is one of the few settlements that has electricity for a few hours most nights.

Yagua Indian Community

The *Yagua* tribe was one of many Amerindian groups that flourished in the northwest Amazon. Long since acculturated due to their proximity to Iquitos, they live much as the other *ribereños* do today. They dress as everyone else, and the children are taught Spanish except in a few bilingual schools where their native language is also used. Yet to demonstrate their culture as it once was, they don the traditional garb of their ancestors for visiting guests.

Men wear skirts of *chambira* palm fiber, while women wear short cotton wrap-around skirts and *chambira* fiber halters. Men also wear a headdress of this same material. The *chambira* fibers are dyed a reddish-orange with *achiote*, which community members may also wear on their body as paint. The image of men wearing what appear to be skirts may have led Francisco de Orellana, one of the first Europeans to see the Amazon, to name the river *"Las Amazonas"*, after the legendary fearsome women warriors of Greek mythology.

One of the largest buildings in a *Yagua* village is the *cocamera*. This large round hut with a high conical thatched roof is used today as a ceremonial center to pay homage to the *Yagua* deity *Mayantú*. In the past, an enlarged version of this structure housed the entire community for defensive purposes.

You may have the opportunity while at the village to barter or purchase *artesanía* and handicrafts made by community members. Know ahead of time however, that the *Yagua* are consummate traders. Baskets, bracelets, crude carvings, and ceramics are among the usual wares exhibited. There may even be items using animal parts such as toucan bills or caiman skulls, but these must be avoided. The *Yagua* are descended from a different culture, where hunting all animals, if they could be of use, is part of everyday life. They are not aware that many of these items would be confiscated by Customs from people returning home. Your part in not purchasing such products will decrease their value as a trade item and discourage the hunting of souvenir specimens.

Fig. 5-14   Yagua Indians prepare to fire their blowguns to demonstrate their accuracy and effectiveness. In many places in the Amazon Basin, firearms and shotguns have replaced the traditional weapons used for hunting.

Fig. 5-15   The cocamera hut is used today as a ceremonial center.

Fig. 5-16   A Yagua man and woman in typical garb made of palm fibers colored with vegetable dye.

Fig. 5-17   Various items are made for trade by the Yaguas, such as these baskets and hammock of palm fiber.

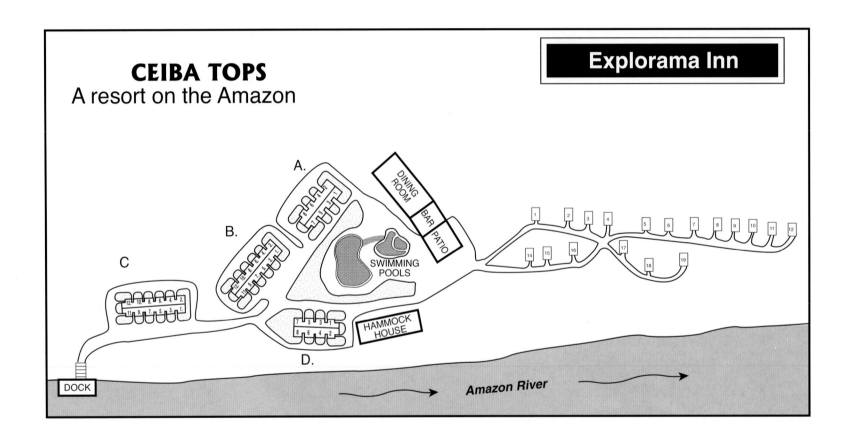

81

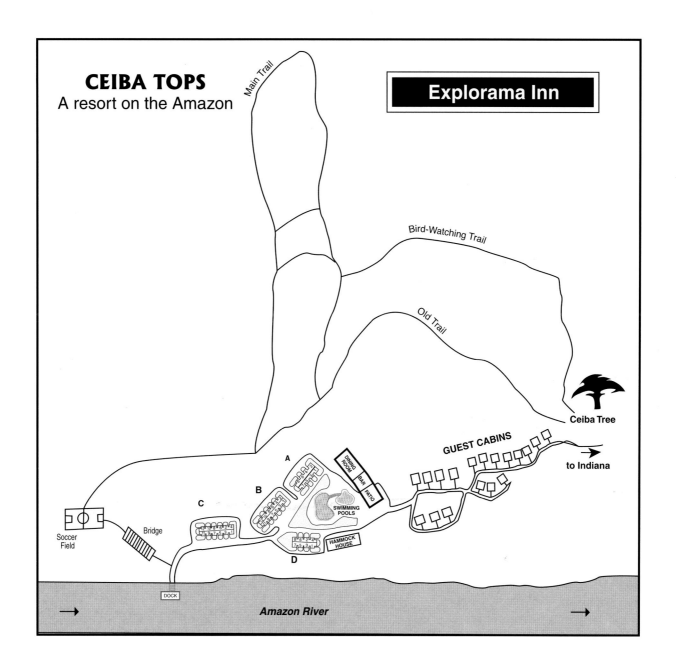

Fig. 6-1   An aerial view of Explorama Lodge nestled within the rainforest of the Bushmaster Reserve. The U-shaped building in the upper left is Casa II and III. Above it is the Hammock House and below it is Casa I. In the middle are the dining hall, kitchen, and employees' quarters. A bridge over Yanacaño stream connects the dining hall with the Tahuampa Bar. Across from the Tahuampa and farthest right in the photograph are more employees' quarters, while behind them is Casa IV. The muddy Yanamono tributary is in the lower right where the boat dock is located.

Chapter 6

Explorama Lodge

Introduction

From the city of Iquitos, Explorama Lodge is only 50 miles down the Amazon River. Explorama's motor launches or *rapidos* cover this distance in one and a half hours (or half that time if you are departing from the Inn or Ceiba Tops). A break in the left bank of the Amazon opens onto a small tributary, or *quebrada*, called the Yanamono, where Explorama Lodge is located. The name is a composite from the Quechua word meaning black (*yana*) and the Spanish word meaning monkey (*mono*). The entrance to the stream is marked by a large isolated clump of bamboo and a larger-than-average dwelling affectionately known as the "rum factory". When the water levels are high, boats turn directly into the *quebrada* while when water levels are low, guests disembark at the riverbank and walk for about 15 minutes to reach the lodge grounds.

If the water is high enough to enter the Yanamono waterway, the launch will slowly negotiate the curvy brown tributary, sliding past children in canoes and women doing laundry at the water's edge. These residents are from the small *Yagua* community called Palmeras which can be seen off the left side of the boat. Along the banks grow large bushes of wild senna with clusters of showy yellow flowers. These flowers are used locally in treating kidney inflammations and are among the herbal remedies sold in the Belen market in Iquitos. Upon arrival at Explorama Lodge, guests are greeted at the Tahuampa Bar and given an orientation and tour of the grounds.

Fig. 6-2   Children from the village of Palmeras play in a canoe along the waters of the Yanamono. Young children in the Amazon Basin learn to paddle almost as soon as they learn to walk.

Facilities

Explorama Lodge is the oldest and largest of the tourist facilities owned and operated by Explorama. Originally constructed in 1965 as a single building, it has grown by gradual additions over the years to a complex of eight interconnected buildings. All have been completely renovated or moved to higher ground during recent years. During the highest water, boats are actually moored at the dining hall and the Tahuampa Bar is reached by a floating balsa walkway.

Using native-style architecture, all of the Lodge buildings have thatched palm-leaf roofs, with columns and braces that are lashed together. Screening was added to the dining room and bar for mealtime and relaxation comfort. Although there is no electricity, the lamplighter fills, cleans, and lights kerosene lamps in each room punctually on a daily basis. Ground-level kerosene "torches" supply light between the Lodge buildings after dark. A large generator does allow for the presentation of slide programs or use of the public address system when large groups are present.

The Lodge has four guest houses with a total of 72 rooms, giving it the capacity to accommodate 150 people. Twin-bedded rooms have curtains, but no screens, and beds are equipped with mosquito nets. Water pitchers, filled daily with river water, and basins are available in each room for washing. Plenty of potable, filtered drinking water is brought in daily from Iquitos and is dispensed from large, cooler-style jugs at each house. Latrine-style bathrooms and gravity-fed showers with cool water are a short walk by covered walkway from each house. Most people find the cool shower water exhilarating in the tropical heat, while others learn to wait until later in the afternoon when the sun has had a chance to warm the water in the storage tank. Although the accommodations initially seem rustic, guests quickly adapt to the environment. After days packed with adventure and physical activities from dawn to dusk, most guests can be found sleeping soundly under their mosquito-nets not long after dinner.

Among the most popular places at the Lodge are the Hammock Houses. These are ideal places to enjoy a light breeze, chat, take a siesta, read a book or write in your journal. Competing with the Hammock Houses in popularity, especially in the evening, is the Tahuampa Bar. Although *tahuampa* means swamp, most guests flock to this watering hole late in the afternoon when the music starts. The walls of

Fig. 6-3   Casa III is one of four guest bungalows at Explorama Lodge. Most structures are on stilts to aid in ventilation and to accommodate the seasonal fluctuation of the river level.

Fig. 6-5   The Lodge dining hall or comedor is screened and has an entrance foyer with books and articles.

Fig. 6-4   A typical open-air room in one of the Lodge bungalows consists of two beds with mosquito nets, shelves, and a table with water pitcher and wash basin.

Fig. 6-6   A set of authentic manguaré drums used by Amerindians for communication. They are struck with mallets made of natural rubber.

87

the Tahuampa are lined with *artesanía* and traditional crafts, while other souvenirs like t-shirts and post-cards can also be purchased. Guides and workmen double as musicians and strum romantic melodies as they sing Spanish songs. As the mood of the audience (or the musicians) becomes more lively, the slow, sensuous chords of *boleros* and *rumbas* give way to the more energetic rhythms of *merengues*, *cumbias*, and *salsas*.

The Forest, Flora, and Fauna

An aerial view of Explorama Lodge shows that it is surrounded by rainforest which offers a unique opportunity for tourists and scientists alike, to have immediate access to its wonders. The Lodge itself is situated at an elevation of about 400 feet. The surrounding forest receives about 140 inches of rain annu-ally, but not in a distinct "wet" and "dry" season. The water levels of the river are more seasonably pre-dictable with the lowest levels occurring from June to January and the highest from February to May. The Lodge is built on the Bushmaster Reserve which encompasses about 250 acres owned by Explorama. It is adjacent to the Yagua Amerindian Reserve with another 4,000 acres of protected tropical forest.

A variety of interesting plants and trees grow on the Lodge grounds. Chocolate trees, for instance, can be found directly behind House III. Their tiny flowers grow in clumps from the trunk and may be easily missed at first glance. The fruit pods however are 6-10 inches long and green, yellow, or red in color. Each contains 20-60 seeds, which when roasted and ground, give us chocolate. The Latin name for this tree genus is *Theobroma,* which translates appropriately as "food of the gods". Also located behind House III is an ivory palm tree. Only 8-10 feet high, this palm produces hard wooden spiny fruits that grow in lumpy clusters at the base of the leaves. When mature, these fruits have hard ivory-like seeds inside. Known as "vegetable ivory" or *tagua*, this material can be carved into figurines or manufactured into items such as buttons.

Growing right alongside the Tahuampa is the calabash tree. If it is bearing fruit, its identity will be obvious as the large rounded shiny green globes may weigh up to 20 pounds. If not, several more of these trees grow behind the house across from the Tahuampa Bar. Calabash shells are used as dippers and

Fig. 6-7   *Music is a constant companion in the Tahuampa Bar where a guitar is never very far away. Musicians, guides, and guests get together almost daily to play, sing, and dance. The most popular rhythms are boleros, rumbas, merengues, lambadas, and cumbias.*

Fig. 6-8   The Tahuampa Bar is the social center of Explorama Lodge. Here it is pictured prior to an addition which doubled its size.

bowls, or used to make carvings such as those displayed in the Tahuampa. Between House IV and the stream which the bridge crosses, you may find heliotrope growing during low water season. The small purple flowers of this plant are extremely attractive to a butterfly group called the glasswings (Family Ithomiidae). The male butterflies attract females via a chemical scent called a pheromone which is released from special patches of scales on the wings. Many of the chemical components necessary to make this butterfly perfume are obtained from the heliotrope. This kind of essential interaction between plant and animal is common in the rainforest ecosystem.

For birding, habitats including the forest edge, small streams, ornamental bushes, and feeders attract a wide variety of birds and other wildlife on the Lodge grounds. The noisiest resident birds, without question, are the macaws. Fed daily with fresh tropical fruits, these giant parrots are continually getting into mischief when not occupying their perch just outside of the dining room. There are usually both blue and gold, and scarlet macaws, always entertaining with their raucous antics. They can also be seen flying over the lodge but return each night to occupy their perches before sunset.

The calls of several other birds are commonplace around the Lodge. A not unmelodious early morning sound is the call of the russet-backed oropendola. Described in one field guide as a "liquid gurgling", thoughts of air bubbles reaching the surface of a water cooler come to mind. These attractive birds weave large, pendant oriole-like nests which are often visible from the balconies of House II and House III. Contributing to the array of unusual bird sounds at the Lodge are the speckled chachalacas. Difficult to describe, their calls are reminiscent of several old cars straining to start at the same time. These drab, pheasant-size birds are shy and tend to stay in the dense thickets where they feed on seeds, fruits, and other vegetable matter. Their cautious nature is adaptive, as chachalacas and other members of this group (guans, currasows) are heavily hunted.

If while dozing under your mosquito net at night you think you hear something flying above you in the rafters, you are probably right. There is no need to be alarmed though, as tropical screech owls include almost all of the lodge bungalows as part of their hunting grounds. These cute owls are barely 10" tall and patrol the upper areas of the bungalows for insects that are attracted to the lamps at night. Large

Fig. 6-9   The fruit from the ivory palm provides a source of "vegetable ivory" also known as tagua.   © SL Timme

Fig. 6-10   The calabash tree produces huge fruits that are scraped and used for dippers or decorative carvings.

Fig. 6-11   A cacao pod produces the seeds that are roasted to make chocolate.

Fig. 6-12   A glasswing or ithomiine butterfly sits on the fruit stalk of a heliotrope plant. Chemicals in the plant are used by the male glasswing butterflies to manufacture sex pheromones.

moth wings are sometimes found scattered on the floor as evidence of their nocturnal feasting. The tropical screech owl's name in Spanish is also its song: cu-ru-cu-cú.

The raised deck platform near the stream passing under the bridge offers a unique vantage point for birds like the sunbittern. This beautiful bird has ornately-patterned plumage and is about the size of a small heron. It is typically found along streams where it catches fish, frogs, and sometimes insects. From time to time it will spread its wings and display the "sunburst" pattern around a central orange spot. Equally as impressive, although much smaller, are the many tanagers that flit to and fro among the bushes along this stream. The crimson-backed tanager is especially impressive with a bright scarlet body and jet black wings.

The Lodge also has its share of resident mammals from time to time, some of which can be seen roaming free throughout the grounds. The tapir or *sachavaca* (wild cow) is one of the most difficult to miss. These prehistoric-looking animals have a long snout that twists around in the air like the much abbreviated trunk of an elephant. Related to the horse and rhinoceros, tapirs are the largest terrestrial mammals in the Amazon Basin and can reach weights exceeding 500 pounds. For this reason they have been hunted extensively and are scarce and extremely wary in areas near heavy human habitation. Young tapirs have white stripes and spots that help them blend in with the dappled light of the forest. Older animals are dark, with short hair that lies close to the skin. These creatures make an absurd, whistle-like noise which seems totally out of place coming from such a massive animal.

Excursions

The Lake Trail

A trail that leads from the Lodge to *Urco Cocha*, a small ox-bow lake, is seasonally inundated. If your visit coincides with low-water season, you can walk with a guide along this interesting looping trail which covers about two miles. Along this trail, as well as throughout the forest, is a strangely undulating vine that is flattened but wavy. This is the monkey ladder vine (*escalera de mono*), which belongs to the

Fig. 6-13   A monkey ladder vine with its wavy and flattened form is a common sight in the forest.

genus *Bauhinia*. The foliage has a deeply split leaf that looks like an animal's hoof. A tree with buttress roots called *capinuri* is also found in flooded forest. Like the kapok, it is an emergent tree. Its unique feature however is the phallic shape of the tips of its fallen branches. A quick search among the leaf litter may yield one or two of these unusual sticks. If your guide can't find any, several are usually on sale as souvenirs at the Tahuampa.

Along the path, you are sure to eventually notice some rounded brown objects on various tree trunks or branches which may range in size from a basketball to the size of a small boulder. These are termite nests with their protected exterior tunnels which can be seen as brown "lines" leading out from the central mass. The brown material is called carton, and is a mixture of chewed wood, saliva, and feces. If one of the tunnels is broken open, you will quickly see dozens of termites attracted to the site of the disturbance. Some will be dark-headed soldiers looking to guard the nest while others will be workers whose efforts to repair the damage will begin almost immediately. Even a small termite nest the size of a bowling ball may easily have as many as 10,000-20,000 individuals making up the colony. Termites are important in the nutrient recycling processes that take place in the forest. Combined with the actions of fungi, they help to break down plant matter, freeing the nutrients and chemical components so they are available again to other organisms.

Fungi are among the least studied and most unappreciated organisms in the rainforest. Their diversity is incredible. There are some that sprout from rotting wood in the form of beautiful red cups, while others take the shape of delicate parasols. Some are luminescent and cast an eerie spectral glow in the jungle's darkness. Others are parasitic killers of insects, invading their bodies and causing their deaths. Beetles and large ants are common targets of these entomophagous fungi. Bracket fungi grow in shelf-like series on fallen trees where brightly-colored, hump-backed beetles may be found in association with them. These pleasing fungus beetles look more like slow-moving pieces of painted and glazed ceramics than they do insects. The beetle larvae feed on the fungal material, often occurring in clusters on the underside of the bracket.

Fig. 6-15   Tiny delicate cup fungi can sometimes be found on decaying wood.

Fig. 6-14   The bracket or shelf fungus is only one of many different groups of fungi found in the rainforest.

Fig. 6-16   The blood mushroom is not a real mushroom or toadstool but rather a root parasite of various trees.

Near the lake is a difficult landmark to miss - - a huge kapok tree. Enormous buttress roots form vertical walls on the lower trunk resembling rocket fins. As the roots reach the ground they become curvy, stretching out from the trunk in a sinuous manner. Although photography of people standing near these buttresses is a tempting jungle "photo-op", snakes have been found curled up at the base of these roots and visitors are advised to look carefully before stepping.

The lake, called *Urco Cocha*, marks an approximate halfway point on the Lake Trail. The *cocha* or lake itself has become a morass of aquatic plants floating in shallow water during low-water season. You can walk out on a fallen log for a better view and will notice that the area is teeming with dragonflies and other kinds of insect life. Bird enthusiasts will be interested in the horned screamers. These large goose-sized birds have a unique morning call which has been variously described as a honk-hoot-squeak. The "horn" in their name refers to a single long quill feather on top of their head. They are found near marshes and swamps where their large, unwebbed feet allow them to walk on top of the vegetation. Horned screamers feed on vegetation and are unique in having an air space under their skin.

From time to time, looking down at your feet may reveal what looks like an animated piece of tire tread. In actuality, they are forest floor millipedes, slow-moving harmless scavengers. Encased in an armored flattened chitinous shell, they curl up in typical millipede defense posture when disturbed. A close look at the legs will show that there are two pair per body segment, unlike their faster and predatory relatives, the centipedes, which only have one pair per segment.

While walking it becomes obvious that at one or two places the canopy seems much more open. This phenomenon is known as a gap, and calls attention to one of the most important environmental factors in the forest - - light! The cause of natural gaps is usually the toppling of a rainforest giant that clears out a swath of trees and vegetation where it lands. Age, disease, and infrequent but violent wind storms contribute to the demise of trees that may have stood for over a hundred years. A treefall-gap does not remain open for long, as dormant seeds quickly germinate in response to the higher light intensity. The ground level quickly becomes occupied as shrubs and small trees begin to grow. As more shade is

Fig. 6-17   Author standing between the buttress roots of
a giant ceiba tree (Ceiba pentandra).

Fig. 6-18   Fruits of a ceiba tree show the red outer
shell and the cottony inner material called kapok.

Fig. 6-19   The forest floor millipede is a slow-moving,
harmless scavenger found among the leaf litter.

produced, the environment is altered once again paving the way for a series of more shade-tolerant plants to take over. In this way succession continues until the gap is eventually filled again with mature forest.

A crashing of branches and some high-pitched chattering announce that monkeys inhabit this forest as well. If you are quiet and look carefully from the proper vantage point, you may be able to spot them silhouetted against the sky. One of the keys for observing primates is quiet (and a good guide). There are six species of monkeys that have been seen at the Lodge. Saddleback tamarins are frequently observed on the Lake Trail, but often also visit the dining hall area to raid the macaws' food dish! Pygmy marmosets and squirrel monkeys are also not uncommon on this trail. The latter travel in large groups ranging from 20-100 individuals and are often seen in the foliage at the edges of rivers and lakes feeding on insects, fruit, and nectar. Squirrel monkeys are 10-12" long with a dark muzzle and crown, and a white mask around the eyes. Their body color is olive-gray, and their long tail is tufted but not prehensile.

One monkey that is heard but rarely seen is the red howler monkey. These large primates reach up to 28" long, have reddish hair, a prehensile tail, and an enlarged throat. Like other howlers, members of a troop will chorus in early morning and late afternoon. The howls and roars of both sexes may be mistaken by some for thunder in the distance. Other monkeys seen at the Lodge are the night monkey and the equatorial saki.

Many other species of mammals are found in the forest within close proximity to the Lodge. Some are only active at night, while others are extremely wary. Poaching on the reserves is a constant problem, in spite of Explorama's efforts to maintain a protected area for the fauna. The paca, for example, is a large rodent that weighs up to 30 pounds. It is nocturnal and forages on fallen fruits and roots. Its meat is prized throughout its range, making it a rare sight in populated areas.

The South American coati is also sometimes seen at the Lodge. It is similar to a raccoon in size and antics, but has a long snout and extremely long ringed tail that is often carried straight up. The fur color tends to be dark brown, but is extremely variable. Coatis are daytime creatures and unusual because they are as at home in the trees as on the forest floor and as likely to be seen alone as in groups of up to 25-30. Coatis eat just about anything including insects, fruit, tubers, and small animals. They spend the night sleeping in the treetops.

Fig. 6-20   The red passion flower is one of more than five hundred species of passion vines that occur in the New World tropics.

Fig. 6-21   *The rainbow katydid is one of more than 80 new species discovered at Explorama's reserves and lodges. The pigments and pattern are probably warning coloration as field experiments have shown this species to be distasteful to its predators.*

At the end of the Lake Trail, you may see what appear to be clumps of low red toadstools. Although named blood mushrooms, they are really not a fungus. These are the flower stalks and inflorescences of a root parasite. They completely lack chlorophyll, which makes them similar in habit and form to the plant known as Indian pipes that grows in the United States. Indigenous people of the Amazon use both the juice and the powder of the blood mushroom as an astringent to staunch the flow of blood.

The Bushmaster Trail

From the highest part of the Lodge begins a trail named after one of the largest and most formidable of venomous tropical snakes - - the bushmaster! Some say this trail was so named due to the high number of bushmasters killed when it was first hacked out of the jungle but the truth is there was only one. Others say it loops and curves around like a snake and that it is the shape of the trail that is responsible for the name. Whatever the historical reason, visitors need not be intimidated but should always be careful. To complete the entire circuit takes 3-4 hours, however your guide will know a number of narrow side paths that criss-cross the main trail and can bring you back to the Lodge in less than two hours.

At the entrance of the trail and near the forest's edge, there are normally several different kinds of passion vine (genus *Passiflora)*. Hundreds of species occur in the Neotropics, many with vastly different leaf shapes. Interesting relationships have evolved between the passion vines and the insect world. Almost all *Passiflora* have structures called extra-floral nectaries. These are small cup-like areas of the plant that are not on the flower, but nevertheless produce a sugary nectar. This nectar attracts ants and wasps which serve to guard the plant against some of its would-be defoliators. There are also poisonous compounds in the plant itself that tend to deter most insects and animals that would feed on its leaves.

Heliconian butterflies (Family Heliconidae) are a widespread neotropical group of insects whose caterpillars feed strictly on passion vines. Instead of being repelled or sickened by the poisons within, the larvae obtain protection by ingesting them. This protection is passed on to the adults in certain species, almost all of which are slow-flying and have contrasting and easily recognizable color patterns. Like the tiny dart-poison frogs, these butterflies advertise their unsavory taste through warning coloration. Other

Fig. 6-22   *The adult tapir is dark in color and may reach a weight exceeding 500 pounds.*

Fig. 6-23   *Baby tapirs have stripes and spots that help to camouflage them in the forest.*

Fig. 6-24   *The agouti is a secretive rodent that feeds on fallen fruits and seeds which aids in their dispersal.*

Fig. 6-25   *A capuchin monkey peers down from a breadfruit tree near Explorama Lodge.*

Fig. 6-27   The bright red bracts of the "hot lips" plant attract hummingbirds to its pale inconspicuous flowers.

Fig. 6-26   A six-foot long boa constrictor observed near the Bushmaster Trail.

Fig. 6-28   Leafcutter ants bring freshly cut booty back to an underground nest.

insects capable of feeding on these plants use the same strategy. The leaf-footed bug, so named due to wide flaps on the hind legs, is a perfect example. One Peruvian species is iridescent green with bright orange and purple leg flaps.

The Bushmaster Trail winds through upland or terra firma forest, incredibly rich in tree species. The late tropical botanist, Al Gentry, worked in this forest for many years and found more than 300 different species of trees on a single 2.5 acre plot. This remains the highest recorded tree diversity in the world. Although the trail begins in an area of secondary growth, the plant composition soon changes as you enter primary rainforest and see large trees and immense lianas.

A white-bearded manakin lek is located not far into the forest. Leks are areas where male birds gather in groups to attract and display for females. The quick bursts of flight of this small manakin create a staccato sound not unlike a sudden discharge of electricity that is difficult to describe, yet unforgettable once heard. Other birds seen along this trail include the black-spotted barbet, a large (6-7") colorful species that is not shy about showing itself. They forage in groups and often join other birds to form mixed-species flocks. Paradise jacamars are sometimes seen sitting on the outer branches of trees. Dark metallic plumage, a white throat, extended tapering tail feathers and a long straight beak make them easy to identify. The spotted puffbird is stockier in appearance, with a larger head and stouter bill. This precocious medium-sized bird feeds on berries and insects, and is often seen perched on low branches.

As you follow the Bushmaster Trail, you may notice shrubs with red lip-like flowers. This plant is commonly known as "hot lips" or "sweetheart lips" for obvious reasons. Like the heliconias, the red parts of the plant are actually bracts while the small white flowers emerge as a cluster in the center between them. Hummingbirds like the fork-tailed woodnymph are attracted to the red color and can be seen flitting from bush to bush, pollinating the tiny flowers. The spectacular purple and emerald-green plumage of this hummer make it an exciting sight. In spite of its small size, it is extremely aggressive and territorial. Also growing amongst the "hot lips" are representatives of one of the most easily identified tropical plant families (Melastomataceae), whose members have three longitudinal veins in each leaf which divide it neatly into four distinct sections.

You will pass countless insects on your trek, many of which will go unnoticed due to their small size or effective camouflage. One of the more prominent groups is the ants. What they lack in size, they make up in sheer numbers. Ants and termites comprise more of the biomass (amount of living material by weight) of a tropical forest than any other animal group. It may be difficult to grasp the concept of ants outweighing a 200-pound capybara or 400-pound tapir, but remember that some ant colonies have more than 10 million individuals!

The sight of leafcutter ants is synonymous with the tropics. Columns of these ants, sometimes more than a foot in width, pass each other as some carry back their fresh cut leaves while others hurry forth to get more. Leaf-cutters live in what can be vast underground nests, sometimes encompassing an acre or more. Tell-tale signs of these nests are surface deposits of the reddish clay-like soil they excavate and refuse piles of old bits of leaves. Indications of the passage of leafcutter ants are the distinctive semicircular areas cut away from the leaves as they harvest them. As long as their shear-like mandibles can cut through it, any accessible plant matter (leaves, stems, flowers, etc.) may be used by the ants. Their foraging may take them up into the tops of trees or be confined to within only a few feet of the ground.

Once a section of leaf is cut out, it is deftly maneuvered into a position where it can be carried. The worker ant then joins her nestmates in a column returning to the nest. Sometimes a smaller ant will even ride back on the newly cut leaf. Once below ground in the nest, the leaf is chopped up not to be eaten but to be integrated into the well-established fungus gardens that are cultivated by the ants. These plots are carefully tended and fertilized with salivary secretions until they produce fruiting bodies which are then consumed by the ants.

Several species of anteaters have been seen on the Bushmaster Trail, from small pygmy anteaters locally called *angelitos* (little angels) to the giant anteater that can hold its own against a jaguar. The giant anteater is a large, powerful beast weighing up to 90 pounds and reaching up to five feet long not including three additional feet of a long shaggy tail. Giant anteaters are restricted to the ground, and are usually seen more in grassland than in rainforest habitat. They amble about with an ungainly gait, walking on their knuckles. The front feet have three huge claws used for ripping open ant mounds, many of which are visited in a single day.

The collared anteater or southern tamandua is considerably smaller than the giant anteater. It rarely reaches a length of three feet, has a light-colored coat with a black "vest", and a naked, prehensile tail. Like the giant anteater, its head extends into a long, narrow snout. Active by day or night, in the trees or on the ground, the southern tamandua forages alone. It eats not only ants, but termites and bees as well, using the four large claws on its front legs to break into nests. These medium-sized anteaters are often seen near streams.

Although on a trail named Bushmaster you would expect to see a snake, in the rainforest one quickly learns that you can not guarantee finding any particular animal. The fer-de-lance, a venomous snake, can sometimes be seen, but it is extremely well camouflaged with a dappled gray-brown pattern. The giant anaconda can attain a length of 30 feet, but is a water snake and seldom seen outside of secluded swampy areas. Boa constrictors, like the emerald tree boa, are also only seen on trails if you are lucky.

As you walk through the forest you are sure to see many huge woody jungle vines called lianas. Some have a girth rivaling trees themselves and a single liana may loop throughout the crowns of many trees. A falling tree and large liana can bring down several other trees in a domino effect. A guide can identify some of the smaller vines which offer a source of water to thirsty travelers. With a quick ringing slice of a machete, a severed vine will drip enough water forced out by gravity for a good drink.

One tree along the Bushmaster Trail bears the scars of many machetes on its trunk. Cutting the bark produces a white sticky sap which can be processed for many different uses. In fact, the industrialized nations of the world would be hard-pressed to survive without it, for it is rubber! Called *caucho* in Spanish, it is probably the most historically important plant in the Amazon Basin. Fortunes were made and thousands of lives lost (almost entirely those of Indians) during the decades that encompassed the rubber boom. Although synthetic rubber is now available, the superior qualities of natural rubber for use in airplane tires and other specialties keep it in constant demand. Harvesting from extractive reserves containing rubber trees is a sustainable use of the forest.

Bird Watching

An early morning bird walk is a great way to start the day. Early morning and late afternoon are the best times of the day to see birds while they are active. Guides lead early morning birding excursions daily along the *Quebrada Yanamono* to the banks of the Amazon or into the forest. Groups may take a large open boat across the river to some of the larger islands and inlets. Numerous species of birds are associated with the open river habitats. Kingfishers are a certainty and may include the Amazon, green, ringed, and pygmy. All bear the typical kingfisher "look" of stout, straight beak and squarish head and can be observed plunging torpedo-like into the water in search of fish. The entrance holes of kingfisher nests, burrows excavated in river banks, continuously dot the earth above the water line.

The swallow-tailed kite is a beautiful bird that even beginners should be able to easily spot on the wing. Almost two feet in length, it has distinctive black and white markings and a long, deeply forked tail. It glides in circles above the water and feeds on flying insects. The yellow-headed caracara is a species often seen perched high atop trees near the river where they can survey adjacent pasture and farm land. This small (16") raptor is omnivorous and will feed on fruit, insects, small mammals, and carrion. The cormorant which feeds on fish and is an expert diver is also a common water bird, greatly resembling the anhinga with its long straight neck.

The Rum Factory

One of the favorite excursions while staying at Explorama Lodge is a visit to the local establishment that distills sugarcane into rum known as *aguardiente*. Located at the confluence of the Yanamono Stream and the Amazon, it is about a 15-minute walk from the Lodge. Along the way, there is a small orchard of mango trees which produce delicious fruit in the months of August and September. Like the cashew tree, mango belongs to the poison ivy family (Anacardiaceae) although touching its leaves generally does not produce a rash. Halfway to the rum factory, you will pass through a gate into a large pasture that extends straight out to the banks of the Amazon River and has several fig trees of impressive height. The white sap of a fig tree has long been used as a purgative in Amazonia, frequently administered to

Fig. 6-29   The heart of the trapiche is the sugarcane press. This trapiche has functioned for over a hundred years. The stacked stems of cane are fed into the rollers which are turned by a horse or mule yoked to the large wooden spar that forms the uppermost portion of the press.

Fig. 6-31   The distillation process is carried out by a picturesque and classic-appearing moonshine still.

Fig. 6-30   The raw sugarcane juice squeezed from the stems is collected in bowls or buckets for processing.

Fig. 6-32   In the manufacture of molasses, raw sugarcane juice is heated in a large copper, wok-like bowl.

children with internal parasites. Throughout the pasture you will also see smaller trees with a reddish peeling bark and smooth reddish or gray-green trunks. These are *capirona* trees which are often used for firewood and the making of charcoal. The pasture itself may or may not be populated by horses, cattle, and even water buffaloes. The latter are part of a government program and tend to spend much of their time shoulder-deep in a small pond near the schoolhouse. Although rather fearsome in appearance, they tend to be docile.

Walking along the banks of the Amazon, you will pass a small homestead above Explorama's low water season docking area. Many useful and fruit-bearing trees are planted around this home, including citrus and cotton which visitors from semitropical areas of the United States may recognize. However, one tree that most people do not recognize, even though they are quite familiar with the edible product it bears, is the cashew.

Cultural differences make themselves apparent in the use of cashews. Most tourists recognize the name from the delicious nuts purchased in the grocery store. To see a cashew developing though is quite intriguing. The C-shaped nut matures in a leathery covering that grows on the bottom of the fruit. The fruit may be yellow or red in color, but is about the size and shape of a bell pepper when mature. Soft and juicy, it is eaten like an apple and used for juice but the nut portion growing from the bottom of this "cashew apple" is discarded by most Amazonian residents. When locals are informed that North Americans eat only the nut, even their polite natures do not keep them from laughing at such folly.

The appearance of rustic soccer goals confirms that the rum factory is near. The first building has firewood neatly stacked around the perimeter and houses the *trapiche* or sugarcane press. Sugarcane is cultivated in fields behind the pasture and the harvested stalks, each surprisingly heavy, are piled next to the *trapiche* for pressing. The *trapiche* looks as if it dates back to the Industrial Revolution, and indeed it is over a hundred years old although it still functions more than adequately, a testament to both fine workmanship and diligent maintenance. Cut sections of cane are fed into the rollers of the *trapiche* which are turned via the efforts of a horse yoked to a massive wooden spar connected to gears on the outside of the rollers. (When a horse is not available, two or three tourists can supply the necessary power for a demonstration!) The sugarcane juice is directed by a spout into waiting buckets while the flattened sections of cane exit the rollers on the other side.

Raw sugarcane juice is used for various purposes. It is a delicious sweet juice to drink right from the *trapiche* or, after a few days, the juice ferments and makes a beer called *huarapo*. Sugarcane juice can also be made into molasses, a process which involves boiling it in a giant copper bowl or wok for a day until it thickens sufficiently. This molasses is used in its liquid form or dried and sold as blocks of brown sugar called *chancaca*. Sugarcane juice is also used for the manufacture of *aguardiente* or sugarcane rum literally translated as "firewater". A vat that looks like an old, deep-sided canoe is filled nearly to the brim with raw cane juice and then left for 20 days to ferment, bubbling and foaming in the process. This liquid is then boiled and distilled in an apparatus that bears every resemblance to an old-time moonshiner's still. The final product is a potent brand of Amazonian "white lightning", which is roughly the equivalent of 150-proof liquor. Some who have sampled it feel that it should be listed way above malaria and venomous snakes as one of the jungle's greatest dangers!

After seeing how *aguardiente* is made, it is only fitting to try some. Next door to the *trapiche* is the home of the owners, Cesar and Socorro Guerra. The front part of their house doubles as a corner store and bar, only in this case it is a corner of the Amazon. They are accustomed to hosting inquisitive *gringos* and Socorro always waves guests up the steps with a smile. She quickly brings glasses over to the table and fills them with the different varieties of rum they make. Usually there is one glass with pure clear *aguardiente*, one with a thicker, brown drink of rum cut with molasses and one with a cloudy concoction of *aguardiente* mixed with ginger root (*ajenjibre*). This ginger root mixture is widely used by *ribereños* for medicinal purposes and is claimed to be the best "bone-warmer" for sufferers of arthritis.

More traditional refreshments such as soda and beer are also available at the Guerra's house and bottles of rum can be purchased "to go" for those who have developed a sudden fondness for it. The rum factory is a comfortable place to enjoy a lazy afternoon partaking of the *aguardiente* that best suits your fancy, enjoying a breeze from the river while listening to Latin music played on a boom-box connected to a car battery, and for those who linger, to enjoy a sunset on the Amazon River as well.

Yanamono Medical Clinic

A short walk from the banks of the Amazon, perhaps a mile in the opposite direction from the rum factory, downriver from the *Quebrada Yanamono*, is "the clinic". Officially christened the Yanamono Medical Clinic, it provides the only medical services available and affordable for many of the inhabitants of the surrounding area. The majority of patients arrive by dugout canoe or on foot, some traveling great distances to reach their destination. The person responsible for the creation of the clinic, and for running it since its inception, is Dr. Linnea Smith, known affectionately as *La Doctora*.

La Doctora

Dr. Linnea Smith first arrived in the Amazon in 1990 for a vacation. Like so many other people who have visited this enchanting environment, it changed her life. A native of Milwaukee, Wisconsin, Dr. Smith graduated from the University of Wisconsin-Madison Medical School in 1984 with board certification in internal medicine. She practiced in Prairie du Sac, Wisconsin, for three years before visiting the Amazon. After only a week's immersion in Amazonian culture, she decided to relocate to Peru. Except for brief trips home to the States, she has been running the clinic and treating indigenous people ever since. She has also chronicled her adventure and life in the Amazon in a book titled *La Doctora* published by Pfeifer-Hamilton Press.

The Clinic

Dr. Smith initially worked out of Explorama Lodge from a room in one of the lodge's thatched-roof houses. She had only the most rudimentary of instruments and held her clinic without electricity, running water, or any staff to help her. Lab services and analyses were out of the question. Medications were donated by kind-hearted tourists before they returned home. Luckily, a Rotary Club member from Duluth, MN, listening to a radio broadcast featuring Dr. Smith changed all that. Volunteers from the Rotary Clubs of Duluth, MN and Thunder Bay, Ontario decided to lend their efforts to her cause. Club members visited the Amazon and built the Yanamono Medical Clinic, purchasing the materials and providing their labor.

Fig. 6-34   *The Yanamono Medical Clinic provides the only medical services available to many of the ribereño people.*

Fig. 6-33   *La Doctora Linnea Smith.*

Today the clinic has three rooms for treatment, plus a laboratory, office, dental room, and pharmacy. Solar panels provide electricity so that flashlights and kerosene lamps no longer need to be used for nocturnal emergencies. A well provides running water and a hammock house is available for family members of clinic patients who need to stay overnight. Perhaps most important, Dr. Smith has been able to train a medical assistant and clinic workers so that a staff of five local residents now supports her efforts.

The long-term goals of the clinic are to expand services, encourage preventative medicine, and promote medical services and family planning in the area. Dr. Smith currently treats about 2,400 patients a year, her practice having grown entirely by word of mouth. Her duties have included treatment of snakebite, cholera, parasites, infectious diseases, malaria, and trauma. Services including family medicine, prenatal care and birthing, and dental care are also provided.

The clinic operates on a minimal budget through support from colleagues, health care professionals, tourists, foundations, organizations, and friends and family. Grants have been provided over the years from a number of different sources. Explorama has provided room, board and river transport for Dr. Smith since she began her work in Peru. Anyone interested in donating to the clinic may do so at the address provided below. The Amazon Medical Project is a registered non-profit organization in the United States and Peru. Volunteer opportunities are also available at the clinic for physicians, PA's, nurse practitioners, and fourth-year medical students.

Donations or inquiries may be sent to:

Amazon Medical Project, Inc.
Rt. 2, 5372 Mahocker Road
Mazomanie, WI 53560
Phone: 608-795-2363
Fax: 608-795-2646
e-mail: amp@amazonmedical.org

Fig. 6-35   A three-toed sloth slowly makes its way up a cacao tree at Explorama Lodge.

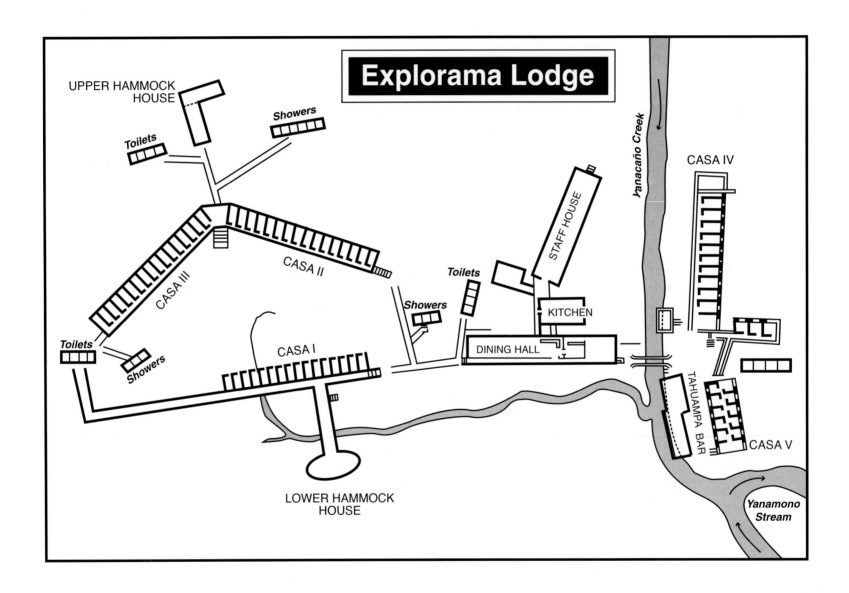

Explorama Lodge

UPPER HAMMOCK HOUSE

Showers

Toilets

CASA III

CASA II

Toilets

Showers

CASA I

Showers

Toilets

LOWER HAMMOCK HOUSE

STAFF HOUSE

Yanacaño Creek

KITCHEN

DINING HALL

CASA IV

TAHUAMPA BAR

CASA V

Yanamono Stream

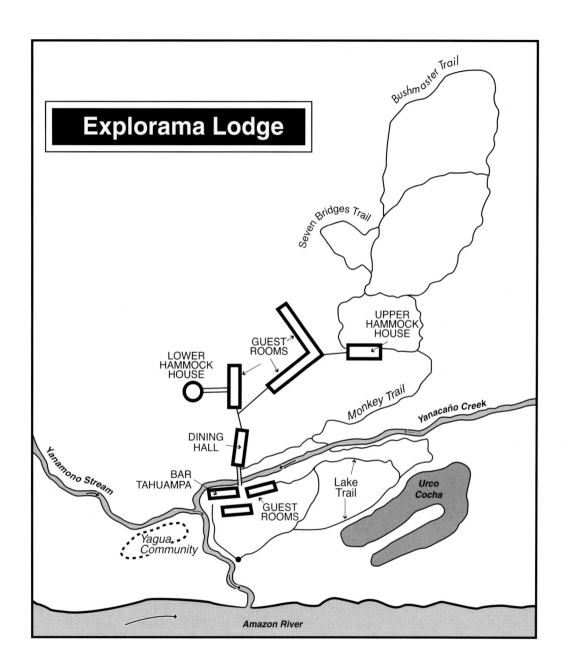

Explorama Lodge

Bushmaster Trail

Seven Bridges Trail

UPPER
HAMMOCK
HOUSE

GUEST
ROOMS

LOWER
HAMMOCK
HOUSE

Monkey Trail

Yanacaño Creek

Yanamono Stream

DINING
HALL

BAR
TAHUAMPA

Lake
Trail

Urco
Cocha

GUEST
ROOMS

Yagua
Community

Amazon River

Fig. 7-1   Aerial view of ExplorNapo Lodge situated on the Sucusari River. This photo was taken prior to extensive construction and additions in 1996.

Chapter 7

ExplorNapo Lodge and ExplorTambos

Introduction

ExplorNapo Lodge is located another 50 miles from Explorama Lodge down the Amazon and up the Napo River. After only a few minutes on the Amazon River during this transfer, Explorama boats normally slow to a stop. It is not engine trouble, but a planned part of the trip. The confluence of the Napo and Amazon Rivers overlooks such an immense quantity of water that it appears as if you are floating on a large sea or ocean. The boatman does not stop just to appreciate the view however, but in hopes that some river dolphins might be present. Both pink and gray dolphins, found in the waters of the Amazon and Napo rivers, feed primarily on fish which congregate where rivers converge. Luckily, they are not hunted in this area because river people believe, according to local legend, that dolphins exit the water in human forms to seduce and interact with villagers.

Of the two species of dolphins, the pink river dolphin is larger (6-8 feet long) and paler in color with a pinkish hue. It often swims alone and tends to show little more than its back when it rises to the surface. Pink dolphins are only found in fresh water. The gray dolphin is smaller (4-5 feet long) and darker above with light gray below. Gray dolphins, found in both fresh and salt water, tend to swim in groups and are much more prone to the Flipper-like displays we associate with dolphins.

After a few minutes on the Napo River, the village of Francisco de Orellana is seen off the left-hand side of the boat. It is named after the famous Spanish explorer who is credited with the "discovery" of the Amazon in 1541. At that time, Orellana was actually trying to discover a food supply that could be brought back to a stranded expedition awaiting his return. He was unsuccessful in rejoining his leader, Gonzalo Pizarro, but wound up traveling some 3,000 miles in ten months from the Napo River to the mouth of the Amazon. Orellana was later made governor of the lands he explored for the king of Spain, but succumbed to fever on his second Amazon venture and died at the age of 35.

The scenery along the Napo River is similar to that of the Amazon. Although a decade ago dwellings were scarce the further away from Iquitos you traveled, nowadays, homesteads can be seen almost continuously. Close to ExplorNapo, the *rapido* slowly veers into a wide *quebrada* off the Napo called the Sucusari. This beautiful stream winds around and provides some of the most spectacular forested scenery. Flowering trees and bushes overhang the water and a profusion of growth along the forest's edge creates a wall of green along the banks.

On the right side of the stream what appears to be a rather large homestead is actually the field headquarters of CONAPAC, the Peruvian organization which has the biodiversity rights to 100,000 hectares (250,000 acres) of primary rainforest located to the east of the Sucusari Stream. Rounding a bend, the high posts supporting ExplorNapo Lodge's sleeping pavilion come into view, and immediately afterward a floating dock marks the entrance to ExplorNapo.

Facilities

ExplorNapo Lodge was constructed on the north bank of the Napo River in 1982. Known then as ExplorNapo Camp, it was by far the most rustic and primitive of all the facilities. Guests slept communally on one large, raised, unscreened platform and the dining area was open-air. Offering the maximum in seclusion, ExplorNapo soon became the favorite place for birding groups led by world-famous ornithologists such as Ted Parker.

With the increasing popularity of the Canopy Walkway, major renovations and changes were made to the Camp so that more guests could experience this spectacular site. A new guest house was constructed and the former dining room was extended and screened. What previously served as the sleeping platform became a hammock house and quarters for the guides. Some may feel that the conversion of

Fig. 7-2   A view of the rear portion of the guest bungalows at ExplorNapo Lodge. The open-air rooms look out on a forested hillside. Visitors have a vista of the Sucusari River from the raised balconies in front.

the Camp to ExplorNapo Lodge, with all of the amenities of Explorama Lodge, has removed some of its rustic charm, but there are now ExplorTambos for those who still yearn for greater privacy and a desire to "be at one" with the forest.

ExplorNapo Lodge has one long house with 20 rooms providing space for 42 guests. Bar service including the "World's Best Pisco Sours on the Sucusari Stream" is available in the large screened dining room where solar powered circular ceiling fans provide a welcome breeze. Some meals, including ExplorNapo's grilled chicken specialty, are cooked on an open-hearth fire.

Forest, Flora, and Fauna

ExplorNapo Lodge is located in a lowland tropical moist forest at an elevation of about 425 feet above sea level. The Explornapo and Sucusari Reserves, which are owned by Explorama, include about 4,600 acres. Also accessible by a short boat ride is the 300-acre Shimigay Reserve. The rainfall in this area normally ranges between 120-160 inches per year, with the highest water levels occurring between December and June while the rivers are lower from July to November. There is both terra firma and inundated forest in the ExplorNapo Reserve.

The rainforest interior at ExplorNapo Lodge is particularly beautiful. While the forest at each of the lodges has its own "look" or "feel" to it, ExplorNapo is somewhat wetter than the others which gives it a more lush appearance. Branches and trunks are often covered with mosses, and plants grow upon plants as tiny epiphylls cover leaves. The forest is filled with hues formed of muted greens and yellows, broken unexpectedly by the contrasting pink of a new palm leaf struck by the sun.

As always, there are many interesting examples of flora and fauna to be found right around the lodge area. A long vine with thick oval leaves, plainly visible from the dining room, hangs from a tree between the kitchen and the bar. Few would guess the plant group to which it belongs or its significance. It is an unusual member of the orchid family, exhibiting a vine-like growth pattern and capable of attaining a length of 80-90 feet. What makes it even more unique is that it is the only orchid of commercial value in the food industry. Material extracted from the seed pod is used as flavorings worldwide.

Fig. 7-3   A vanilla orchid grows outside the dining hall at ExplorNapo Lodge.

Fig. 7-4   Showy inflorescence of the flag tree with red bracts and yellow flowers, growing adjacent to the Hammock House. © Stephen L. Timme

Fig. 7-5   *A capybara, the world's largest rodent, is often found domesticated as a pet at ExplorNapo Lodge. Adults may weigh as much as 200 pounds when full grown. The feet are partially webbed which is an advantage in the swampy, aquatic habitat in which they usually live.*

If you haven't guessed its identity, it is vanilla! The need to hand-pollinate the flowers in cultivation, followed by a lengthy fermentation process of the bean or fruit, is responsible for the high cost of the final product.

Adjacent to the Hammock House are several trees with spectacular red and yellow foliage and flowers. These are flag trees, a subcanopy species which like the heliconia and the "sweetheart lips" are pollinated by hummingbirds. The other trait it shares with those plants is that the bright red leaf-like structures are bracts, not flower petals. The root of the flag tree has many uses in traditional medicine, including being worn around the neck as a perfume and aphrodisiac.

Excursions

Camp Trail

Stretching between ExplorNapo Lodge and the ACEER field station is the Camp Trail, which has split logs used on the ground to prevent trail deterioration. One of the first plants you may recognize on this trail, due to the characteristic three-veined oval leaf, is a melastome. The base of most of these leaves where it attaches to the stem, is swollen and almost bubble-like in nature. This swelling is a domatia and serves as a house or nest for a colony of ants that live on and in the plant. If sliced open, the domatia would reveal many ants at various stages of development. These ants protect the host plant by attacking intruders that would feed on its leaves. In turn, the melastome provides the insects with a place to live, and in some cases also with nutrients in the form of specially-produced carbohydrate packets. When two different species live in a close interdependent association like this one, it is called symbiosis. Where both parties benefit, the relationship is known as mutualism.

You may also come upon another group of very common and famous rainforest ants along this trail. Like the piranha, army ants (*Eciton* spp.) have a much maligned reputation that exaggerates their danger to man. Several species occur and you may see individuals that are dark-bodied and almost black or others that are red. Depicted in movies as unstoppable hoards capable of annihilating anything in their path, the truth is somewhat less dramatic. A person can step a few paces to one side in order to safely avoid their line of destruction. Most human jungle inhabitants live in easy association with army ants and even welcome their visits as an opportunity to rid dwellings of noxious insects with only minor inconvenience.

An army ant colony may have millions of individuals whose members, nearly blind, operate primarily by tactile and chemical cues. There is a single queen which controls whether or not the colony is in a nomadic or sedentary phase. When young ants are developing and need to be fed, the workers fan out or exit in columns to forage. Food consists mainly of insects which are overwhelmed through sheer ant numbers or attacked by soldier ants with long, curving mandibles that resemble ice tongs. According to some accounts, Amerindians used these soldier ants as "living sutures" for cuts by allowing one mandible to hook in on one side of a wound and then the other mandible to hook in on the other side. When the ant bit, the two sides were drawn together and the insect's body was pinched off to leave the head embedded like a staple.

Army ant colonies have no physical nests and utilize available shelter. The queen is protected by the living bodies of tens of thousands of workers that form a mass around her called a bivuoac. This usually occurs in a protected area such as beneath a log or amongst tangled tree roots. The bivuoac is moved daily during the nomadic phase, but may stay in place for two weeks or more when the ants are sedentary.

Following the split logs, you will see palm trees near the path whose bases are formed of stilt-like roots. Two species of these stilt palms, *pona* and *huacrapona,* are used as flooring in most native dwellings. The outer bark is stripped off in one piece and then flattened and fastened down to serve as a floor. Another common palm has dense rings of long sharp black spines that cover the length of the trunk. This palm belongs to the genus *Astrocaryum* which contains the species known locally as *chambira*. The *chambira* fiber is used in weaving hammocks, bags, and other items.

A considerable amount of research on monkeys has been conducted in the forest surrounding ExplorNapo Lodge. Primate researcher Suzi Leonard is affiliated with the Detroit and Dallas Zoos and has spent years roaming the Explornapo and Sucusari Reserves with volunteers from zoos throughout the United States, documenting the behavior of monkey troops. Some species are rare such as the wooly

Fig. 7-6   *The bubble-like swelling at the base of this leaf is a domatia, where a colony of ants lives.*

Fig. 7-7   *The soldiers of some species of army ants have huge curved mandibles used for defense of the colony.*

Fig. 7-8   *Bright-colored caterpillars abound in the forest and usually have stinging spines.*

Fig. 7-9   *The giant ceiba borer has a metallic sheen and can often be found where fallen logs ooze sap.*

Fig. 7-10   *The pristine forest at ExplorNapo Lodge and the ACEER has a wet, lush appearance and special beauty all its own. In the right side of this photo are irapay palms commonly used for roof thatch.*

monkey and both the brown and white-fronted capuchins. Others are seen or heard with great frequency, including the pygmy marmoset, black-mantle and saddleback tamarins, the red and the yellow-handed titi monkeys, the red howler, night monkey, and monk saki. Visitors wishing to observe monkeys should remember that primates must be approached quietly or they will go into hiding or stay so still that they are impossible to see.

Titis are smallish monkeys, only 12-16" high and two to three pounds in weight. Their tails are longer than their body and quite shaggy. They are arboreal and usually travel in small groups of two to five individuals. Their diet varies among species, but may include fruit, insects, and even leaves. Titis can move with great stealth and may be difficult to see, although they produce whooping vocalizations around dawn. The black-mantle tamarin is smaller than the titis, only reaching 8-10" in height and barely a pound in weight. The front half of the animal is black with a white muzzle while the back half is reddish-brown. Of the marmosets and tamarins, this is the only species that will travel in large groups of up to forty individuals. The black-mantle tamarin feeds primarily on large insects such as katydids and grasshoppers but will also eat fruit and nectar.

The monk saki is a larger species of monkey, ranging from 16-20" in length and weighing up to six pounds. It has long shaggy fur and an extremely bushy non-prehensile tail that is at least as long as its body. Traveling in groups of three or four, monk sakis are found primarily in the middle to upper layers of the rainforest where they feed on fruits, leaves, seeds, and even ants. They prefer densely foliated areas of the forest and can sit quietly without moving for long periods of time.

Many other mammals such as the collared anteater and tayra are also found in the ExplorNapo forest. Tayras belong to the weasel family and can reach a length of 28" and a weight of 15 pounds. Their head is usually light-colored and contrasts sharply with the dark body, legs, and tail. They are active primarily during the day, but are sometimes seen at dawn and dusk as well. They are ferocious little carnivores and will feed on birds, mammals, insects, and fruit. Although fairly common, they are wary animals and for this reason are difficult to see.

Mammals more commonly seen at night are porcupines and armadillos. Several species of each occur in the area. Porcupines have been frequently sighted on the Canopy Walkway at night. Attracted to the salt-containing sweat left by visiting tourists on the wooden handrails and platforms, these spiny animals then gnaw on the wood. The result of this gnawing is especially evident on the benches of the walkway's access and departure towers. Porcupines are arboreal and have a prehensile tail that is bare at the tip. In contrast, armadillos are terrestrial and have armor plates instead of barbed spines for protection. They feed primarily on insects such as termites and ants, but will opportunistically take almost anything they can easily overpower. They forage in the litter of the forest floor using their long nose and keen sense of smell. With poor eyesight, they are sometimes oblivious to their surroundings and startle unsuspecting visitors when they suddenly decide to flee.

Bird Watching

ExplorNapo Lodge has long been a bird watcher's paradise by simultaneously providing incredible diversity with ease of accessibility to isolated and undisturbed habitats. It was a favorite haunt of the late Ted Parker, one of the leading experts on Peruvian birds, who brought ornithology classes to the lodge and trained many of the Explorama guides. These same guides, some of whom have led birding excursions for more than 20 years, have an incomparable knowledge of the rainforest birds, their habits, and especially their calls. The additional opportunities now provided by the Canopy Walkway make birding at ExplorNapo Lodge a unique and unforgettable experience.

Parrots are easy to hear with their raucous squawking as they pass overhead, but are somewhat more challenging to see amongst the foliage. The yellow-headed, black-headed, cobalt-winged, and the mealy are all parrot species that inhabit the area. Of course, the most impressive of all parrots are the macaws. On occasion, standing quietly on a canopy platform will reward you with a view of these huge, vividly colored birds as they fly by with their long impressive tails streaming behind.

The cotingas are a group of medium-sized birds about 7-8" in height. Though they cannot compare to macaws in size, their plumage is equally spectacular. The spangled cotinga has turquoise body feathers with a reddish-purple throat and breast. Many birders have come to ExplorNapo exclusively to see the elusive black-necked red cotinga in its lek or display area found along the trail between ExplorNapo and the ACEER. The collared trogon, a larger bird belonging to a different group, also vies for attention with iridescent green feathers above, red feathers below, and black and white plumage on the wings and tail.

Some species are more often heard than seen. The screaming piha, although plain gray in appearance, emits a call at a volume that seems to carry for miles. Almost any visitor to ExplorNapo Lodge or the Canopy Walkway is sure to hear the "pee-pe-yó" call of the screaming piha. An equally common nocturnal counterpart is the "hoo-hoo" call of the spectacled owl. Both species provide easily recognizable calls for the beginning birder.

Medicinal Plant Garden

Just a short walk over the bridge behind the guest rooms exists a treasure trove of ethnobotanical information. The ReNuPeRu Garden is a four-acre plot of land that is carefully tended and holds nearly 200 different species of herbs and trees that have medicinal or other traditional uses. The plants by themselves would be useless however without the information about their preparation and use. This special knowledge has been acquired over the past 40 years by the garden's curator, Antonio Montero Pisco.

Antonio is a *curandero* or shaman, the Spanish word for traditional healer. He began his study of jungle plant lore under the tutelage of his grandparents while a young boy. He is now an expert, not only in the preparation and use of rainforest herbs, but in their cultivation as well. As you look around, you can see the flourishing results of his efforts. There are trees, shrubs, and beds of herbaceous plants, as well as trails into the primary forest where other medicinal plants are found.

The book, *A Field Guide To Medicinal And Useful Plants Of The Upper Amazon*, describes most of the plants cultivated in this garden. *Ayahuasca*, the visionary vine, is used in tribal rituals and by witch doctors (*brujos*) or shamans to commune with the spirit world. *Curanderos* also sometimes use *ayahuasca* to help them diagnose the illnesses of patients who have come to them for help. The plant itself is a large woody vine whose bark is boiled with plant additives to form *ayahuasca*, a powerful

Fig. 7-11   Shaman and curandero Antonio Montero Pisco (left) prepares to give a lecture on medicinal and useful plants to a group of tourists at the ReNuPeRu Medicinal Plant Garden. Senior guide Roldan Hidalgo assists in the translation.

Fig. 7-12 *The visionary vine, ayahuasca, is used by shamans to communicate with the spirit world.*

Fig. 7-13 *Uña de gato or cat's claw vine received its name because of the paired claw-like tendrils.*

Fig. 7-14 *The sap from the dragon's blood tree is used topically to promote healing of wounds.*

Fig. 7-15 *The angel's trumpet plant is a hallucinogen and one of the additives used in making ayahuasca.*

Fig. 7-16   *Wild senna is a common plant often seen along streams. Its flowers are used to treat liver disorders.*

Fig. 7-17   *One of the most important plants in South America is coca, from which cocaine is extracted.*

Fig. 7-18   *The seeds of achiote are used to make a red-orange dye and body paint used throughout the Amazon.*

Fig. 7-19   *The juice squeezed from huito fruits is used to create a blue-black dye and body paint.*
© Stephen L. Timme

hallucinogen known to cause visions. Antonio lectures about many of the plants growing in the garden that he and his son tend. He speaks with a great respect for traditional ways and warns against the use of medicines like *ayahuasca* for recreational purposes. He also advises against false shamans who prepare *ayahuasca* and hold ceremonies just for tourists. Tourists tempted to try it should know that it has also been used medically for decades as an emetic, causing intense diarrhea and vomiting.

At the entrance to the garden is *uña de gato* (cat's claw), another climbing jungle liana. It is named after its distinctive paired tendrils that resemble the claws of a cat. The plant is one of several rainforest species that have seen extensive commercialization and marketing in the industrialized world. It is found in health food stores as pills, in liquid form, and as a tea, and is advertised as a panacea for all types of ills from cancer to AIDS.

Near Antonio's house stands a dragon's blood tree locally called *sangre de grado*. When the bark of the tree is cut a red resin oozes from it explaining the origin of its name. This resin has long been known to possess beneficial properties, and two drugs derived from it are currently in clinical trials. In the Amazon area the sap is used both to staunch the flow of blood and to promote the healing of wounds.

Throughout the garden most of the plants and trees are labeled with a small sign at their base bearing the scientific name. To most visitors however, neither the scientific name nor the plant itself will be recognizable even though its product is familiar. A member of the hibiscus family, a cotton tree bears dried bolls with fluffy white material. In another planter is a *cocona* bush with orange, tomato-sized fruits and small star-shaped flowers. The foliage resembles that of an eggplant, and along with the tomato and potato, the *cocona* belongs to the nightshade family (Solanaceae). *Cocona* provides one of the various fruit juices served at the lodges for breakfast.

Coca has a very bad reputation due to the abuse of the drug cocaine made from the alkaloids in the leaves. For thousands of years coca leaves have been cultivated and used by Andean Native Americans to increase stamina, while decreasing fatigue and hunger. These are useful attributes for people who live in a physically-demanding, high-altitude environment. The leaves also have a high caloric value and are among the richest in calcium of any plants, a useful quality where few milk products are available.

Fig. 7-20   A group of tourists paddle through the dark waters of Lake Shimigay in a dugout canoe in search of the unique hoatzin bird.

Fig. 7-21   The morpho is the quintessential tropical butterfly. Its bright blue is only on the inside of the wings.

Fig. 7-22   The beetle-pollinated flower of the giant Amazon water lily.

Fig. 7-23   The leaves of these large tree-like philoden-drons make up the primary food of the hoatzin bird.

Fig. 7-24   The unusual hoatzin is a bird that is mainly vegetarian and whose young have claws on their wings.
© Andrew W. Kratter

The amount of active chemical consumed by a South American native in a day is only about one one-thousandth of the amount used by a cocaine addict in the same period of time. Unfortunately Antonio has had to remove the sign identifying the coca bush in the medicinal plant garden because so many tourists insisted on trying the leaves themselves. The traditional method of use requires that mineral lime or ash be chewed at the same time in order to release the alkaloid chemicals in the leaves.

Few visitors leave the ReNuPeRu Medicinal Plant Garden untouched, but some show the signs of their visit more visibly than others. The two most common vegetable dyes used as body paint in the Amazon grow in the garden and are employed liberally by Antonio and the Explorama guides. Thus, returning tourists often bear the ochre-colored markings on their face of *achiote* and blue-black temporary "tatoos" on their arms produced by *huito*.

The ReNuPeRu Medicinal Plant Garden and Antonio's efforts have been made possible by the generous donations and support of world-renowned ethnobotanist Dr. Jim Duke. Recently retired from a career of searching for and screening medicinal plants to fight cancer, Jim Duke continues to travel the world in an effort to inform people and increase our knowledge of healing herbs. He is often a visitor at the garden where he gives field workshops on the use of medicinal plants.

Lake Shimigay

The Shimigay Reserve is a half hour boat ride out of the winding Sucusari and up the Napo River. The reserve is named after Lake Shimigay, a tranquil black water lake that may offer the opportunity to see one of the most unusual birds alive - - the hoatzin! During low water, the lake is reached by an hour-long hike from the Napo while during high water, large open canoes can reach the lake directly. In a canoe you must thread through narrow waterways that are often enclosed overhead. On this trip you truly get the feeling for the grandeur of the tropical rainforest as your canoe slowly passes immense trunks laden with epiphytes and branches supporting huge philodendrons and bromeliads. For a short while you can share the sensations that early explorers must have experienced in such a unique environment so far from home.

Tiny dragonflies and damselflies with exotic patterns on their wings often keep pace with boats and a sudden brilliant flash of blue may herald the arrival of a morpho butterfly. The intense cobalt coloring of their wings is actually produced by the diffraction of light off of the scales on the upper surface rather than a pigment in the wings themselves. Decades ago, these wings were sought by industrialized nations and used as the backing in jewelry pieces. Some Indian tribes believe these butterflies represent the spirits of those deceased. The under surface of the wings are brown and dull, an excellent camouflage used while they are at rest with their wings closed. It also makes it extremely challenging to follow the insect's progress while flying, for there are only brief flashes of color followed by their apparent disappearance.

Around the last turn, you emerge into the bright sunlight and upon the still, dark waters of Lake Shimigay. Quiet and slow-moving waters are the favored haunts of the bottom-dwelling electric eel. Actually a fish, it is capable of generating a current that can stun a human being. Used as a method of prey capture and defense, deaths have occurred as a result of electric eels, but usually due to the drowning of a paralyzed victim and not due to electrocution.

Hanging from one of the tree branches near the entrance to Shimigay is a long, gray cylindrical object which upon inspection with binoculars proves to be a wasp nest. Totally enclosed except for a small entrance hole, the colony's young develop in combs stacked like dinner plates inside the nest. Unfortunately, many of the largest of these nests have been removed and brought to shops in Iquitos where they are sold as curios.

Like Lake Yanayacu at the Inn, Shimigay has giant *Victoria amazonica* lily pads. When they first reach the water's surface they appear to be almost rolled in half. Another peculiar plant, although more like a tree, grows directly in the lake. It has large arrowhead-shaped leaves and is a member of the philodendron family (Araceae). It grows abundantly in swampy areas and has a primitive, almost primeval look about it.

Perhaps the most unusual occupant of Lake Shimigay is the hoatzin, a large crested bird about the size of a pheasant. Typically wary and difficult to see, they flap clumsily in the trees along the edge of the lake, grunting their displeasure. Hoatzins could be considered the ruminants of the avian world for their diet consists of over 80% leaves. The foliage of philodendrons, which contains noxious secondary compounds, is usually selected. Hoatzins slowly digest these leaves via fermentation in their crops with the aid of bacteria that live there. The decomposing vegetable matter within renders their meat unpleasant for human consumption and also gives them a rather nasty smell earning them the nickname of "stink birds". Hoatzins build a rather sloppy nest of sticks loosely arranged in the branches of vegetation above the water. They are communal breeders with as many as seven individuals caring for a single nest. Young

Fig. 7-25   In an ExplorNapo tradition, each group of visitors leaves a plaque commemorating their visit. The most creative of such plaques are displayed for the enjoyment and inspiration of future groups.

hoatzins flee from danger by diving into the water. Their ascent back up into the bushes is aided by claws on the wings, an attribute unique in the bird world and only exhibited by the juveniles. Fossils 120 million years old of the first known bird, *Archaeopteryx*, coincidentally show a similar feature. No taxonomic relationship is implied however, as hoatzins appear to be most closely related to the cuckoos.

Night Canoe Ride

With darkness, a change comes over the rainforest as nocturnal creatures begin their period of activity. A variety of sounds occur whose origin may be amphibian, insectan, mammalian, or avian in nature. To the untrained ear it is difficult to identify the source of such vocalizations. Armed with flashlights, it is a wonderful experience to slowly and silently paddle along the Sucusari, scanning the foliage for movement or eyeshine. Eyeshine at water level may indicate a caiman, the South American equivalent of an alligator. Once plentiful, these reptiles have been heavily hunted and it is difficult to see a large specimen today. Reflections from animal eyes in the trees could be many things including a large bird like the great potoo or foraging mammals like a night monkey or kinkajou.

The eyes of a kinkajou will shine with a bright orange glare when struck by a flashlight beam. Like the coati, the kinkajou is a member of the raccoon family, however, it has a rounded head and short pointed muzzle that gives it an almost cat-like appearance. Kinkajous are reddish-brown in color and grow to almost two feet in length not including its long, tapering prehensile tail. Kinkajous inhabit the forest canopy where they feed primarily on figs, and to a lesser extent, on insects. They are most often spotted high in a tree.

The night or owl monkey gets its names from its nocturnal habits and its large, rounded close-set eyes. Although often found near human settlements, they are shy by nature and will not long remain in a flashlight beam. Coloration varies, but their fur is short and they have a long, hairy non-prehensile tail with a black tip. Night monkeys are usually found in the upper levels of the forest. They move quietly as they feed on insects, fruits, and nectar. They range from 10-20" long and weigh up to three pounds.

When passing a stand of bamboo at night, be sure to look for the Amazon bamboo rat, locally known as the *cono cono*. This arboreal rodent reaches about a foot in length and can be identified by its large square muzzle and naked tail. They feed on bamboo shoots, sometimes leaving telltale holes in the stems. The call of the Amazon bamboo rat is heard frequently in the early evening and sounds very much like a frog. These creatures are sometimes active in the late afternoon as well as at night.

On a clear night, regardless of the animal life observed, one display is always spectacular - - the stars! Few scenes rival the Milky Way when viewed on a clear night from an open boat on the river. The absence of any ambient light allows for one of the clearest views of the stars and constellations ever seen. Shooting stars are commonplace. The trajectory of satellites can be easily followed and predicted along their paths for those knowledgeable enough to recognize them. Astronomy buffs quickly make themselves known as the Southern Cross and other constellations of the Southern hemisphere are spotted. The nocturnal Amazon skyscape is unforgettable and something everyone should experience.

ExplorTambo Camp

For those who shun the luxuries of civilization and prefer to be more at one with nature, a visit to ExplorTambos is perfect. Located in the Sucusari Reserve, ExplorTambo Camp is a two hour walk through primary rainforest from ExplorNapo Lodge. Accommodations are available for a maximum of 16 explorers in 8 raised-platform, thatch-roofed shelters called *tambos*. Mattress pads, bedding and mosquito nets complete each shelter. Meals are cooked on an open hearth and served picnic style in the central area of the camp. Bathing is done in a cool water stream that passes by the camp site or hanging solar showers are also available.

Due to ExplorTambo's isolation, the possibilities of spotting wildlife are much better than from any other lodge. Within hiking distance is a naturally occurring *colpa*. This is a mineral watering hole used by forest animals and provides the best opportunity to see mammals. Although spotting mammals is exciting, the best part of a stay at ExplorTambos is sleeping completely surrounded by the sounds of the forest and waking with the birds just outside your mosquito net.

Fig. 7-26   The gray-winged trumpeter is a chicken-like bird that is easily domesticated.
© Stephen R. Madigosky

Fig. 7-27   This young spectacled owl is one of the many species of tropical birds found at ExplorNapo Lodge.
© Stephen R. Madigosky

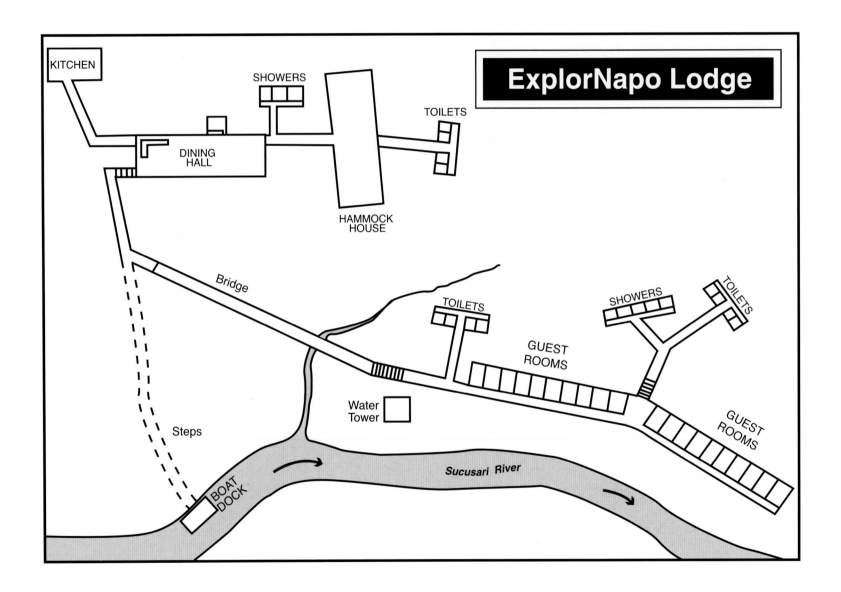

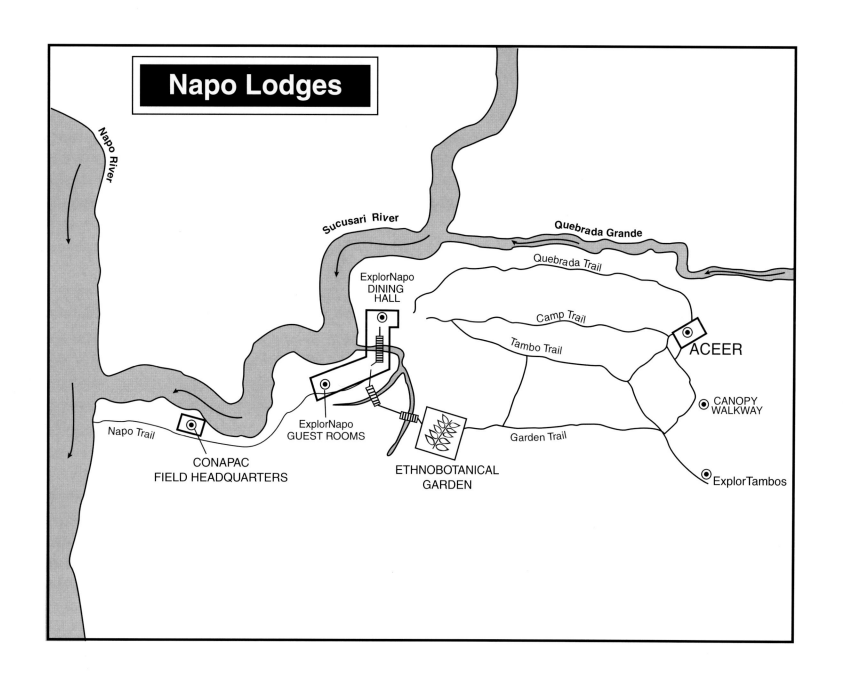

Napo Lodges

Napo River

Sucusari River

Quebrada Grande

Quebrada Trail

Camp Trail

Tambo Trail

ExplorNapo
DINING
HALL

ACEER

CANOPY
WALKWAY

ExplorNapo
GUEST ROOMS

ETHNOBOTANICAL
GARDEN

Garden Trail

ExplorTambos

Napo Trail

CONAPAC
FIELD HEADQUARTERS

Fig. 8-1   Aerial view of the Amazon Center for Environmental Education and Research (ACEER) taken before the construction of the Alwyn Gentry Research Laboratory.

Chapter 8

CONAPAC, ACEER
and the
Amazon Canopy Walkway

Introduction

CONAPAC is an acronym for Conservación de la Naturaleza Amazónica del Perú A.C. (Association for the Conservation of the Peruvian Amazon). It is a Peruvian based non-governmental, non-profit organization that was established in 1990 to receive donations and put them to work in the Peruvian rainforest. CONAPAC currently holds the biodiversity rights to the 250,000 acre CONAPAC Reserve located in the area to the north and east of the ExplorNapo Reserve, the Canopy Walkway and the ACEER field station. In Peru, CONAPAC administrates and organizes the joint CONAPAC/ACEER "Adopt-A-School" program currently providing school supplies to over 3,000 children in 35 rural communities. CONAPAC is also an active participant in a joint program with the ACEER and Iquitos Board of Education to bring conservation education to rural rainforest schools. Many university students also receive scholarships provided by CONAPAC to study various aspects of rainforest biology.

The ACEER Foundation is a U.S.-based non-governmental, non-profit organization which accepts donations used toward educational programs, the construction and outfitting of the ACEER field station and its facilities, as well as other projects in the Iquitos area. The field station also called the ACEER, Amazon Center for Environmental Education and Research, is a 45-minute walk from ExplorNapo Lodge.

The center's purpose is to further the conservation and study of rainforests by disseminating information and providing educational opportunities which include access to tropical forests. Students and visitors can participate in field courses and programs where scientists conduct actual field studies. The name "ACEER" is used to refer to the field station in Peru, the foundation in the United States, and its branch office in Iquitos.

ACEER Field Station

The ACEER consists of a large, screened room which is part dining hall, library, hammock house, and work area. The visitors quarters, two wings of 10 double rooms each, are built on either side of a central social area and have the same facilities as ExplorNapo and Explorama Lodge. The recent installation of solar panels now provides electricity for room lights in some of the buildings.

The Alwyn Gentry Research Laboratory, two large screened rooms with research tables, offer scientists and long-term researchers a place to store their equipment and to do work with specimens that can not be done in the field. Tables, benches, lights, blackboards, and a slide projector also make these facilities useful for holding classes, giving presentations, or conducting training workshops. The ACEER field station has hosted courses in tropical biology and tropical agriculture presented in conjunction with the Organization for Tropical Studies (O.T.S.), which has conducted similar training in Costa Rica for over thirty years. The ACEER lab is named after the late Dr. Al Gentry, tropical botanist extraordinaire, who did extensive botanical research throughout the New World tropics, and had worked with the Missouri Botanical Garden for over 20 years on scattered plots in the Explorama-owned reserves.

Fig. 8-2   A guest bungalow of the ACEER while under construction.

Fig. 8-3   The guest bungalow of the ACEER after completion.

Fig. 8-4   The dining hall and activity area of the ACEER before it was screened.

Fig. 8-5   The buildings that make up the Alwyn Gentry Research Laboratory at the ACEER Field Station.

Trails at the CONAPAC Reserve and ACEER Field Station

Medicinal Plant Trail

This trail extends for over a mile from the ACEER Field Station and provides an opportunity to see many medicinal and useful plant species growing in the wild. The majority of these are trees in their natural state and of much greater maturity than similar specimens cultivated in the ReNuPeRu Medicinal Plant Garden.

Two plants which grow along this trail contribute to the ingredients of perhaps the most famous jungle poison known to man - - curare. They are *Sacha ampihuasca* (*Curarea toxicofera*), a liana with a flattened stem, and *Huasca sanango* (*Strychnos panurensis*), a shrubby tree. Typical preparations use the bark, although stems and seeds may be used with the *Strychnos* spp. as well. Curare has been used by Amerindian groups throughout northern South America for centuries to tip their arrows and blowgun darts used for killing game. The contents often vary from region to region, where a variety of botanical and animal additives may be used. Among the latter are the toxins extracted from the small brightly colored dendrobatid frogs, as well as the venom from the large, predatory bullet ant (genus *Paraponera*).

Curare inhibits neuromuscular activity, preventing nerve impulses from reaching the muscles resulting in paralysis and eventual death due to respiratory failure. Curare does not affect heart action however, and has found widespread applications in medicine as a muscle relaxant. Its use decreases the amount of anesthesia necessary, lowering in turn the negative side effects and associated risks during operations. It makes possible delicate surgery where complete muscle relaxation is essential.

Another tree along the trail used by native Amerindians is *cumala blanca* (*Virola pavonis*). This species, along with others in the genus *Virola*, are used to make a powerful hallucinogenic snuff. Derived from the powdered scrapings of the inner bark, the final product is blown with considerable force into one nostril via a long grass tube. In some cases, the snuff is self-administered by means of a hollow V-shaped bird bone set in a reservoir of the powder.

Huambe (*Philodendron solimoesense*) is an epiphytic plant found growing on the branches or trunks of supporting trees. Like other philodendrons, it sends down long, ropy aerial roots. When harvested, these roots can be used to fasten and hold beams together or as the raw material for making crude baskets.

Two books which describe many of the botanical specimens found along this trail and in the ReNuPeRu Medicinal Plant Garden are the *Amazonian Ethnobotanical Dictionary* and *A Field Guide To Medicinal And Useful Plants Of The Upper Amazon* which also has color photos (see References).

Bridge Trail

Beginning at the front of the ACEER station, the bridge trail is named for the suspension bridge crossing the *Quebrada Grande* stream. During high water season, small boats can enter by this stream providing an alternate route for arriving at the field station. Along this trail you may recognize many plants used as house plants or ornamentals at home. Dieffenbachias, also known as dumbcane, contain oxalic acid crystals which cause the tongue to swell if ingested. The prayer plant (genus *Myranta*) is commonly found on the forest floor and gets its name from the manner in which the leaves fold together at night. Philodendrons are another common group with over 200 species, many of which can be seen along the bridge trail. Some species may appear to be two different plants due to the vastly different leaf size and shape found from one part of the plant to another. Using a tree for support, philodendrons climb with small, heart-shaped leaves closely pressed to the trunk. Once reaching a certain level of light intensity, the leaves change their morphology and become much larger and less symmetrical. In the rainforest, the "fight for light" is a constant battle for plants on the forest floor and many strive to reach the canopy where most of this all-important energy source is located.

Species of trees and bushes in the Piper family (Piperaceae) have slender white fruit stalks that stand upright from their branches. This family includes the common black pepper of commerce. The stalks are harvested by bats which feed on the tiny granular fruits. Given the rapid metabolism of these flying mammals, the seeds quickly pass through their digestive system and are defecated (often in flight).

In this way, bats play an important role as seed dispersers and are key agents in the regeneration of rainforests in disturbed areas.

While walking along bridges in the rainforest, it is always wise to make sure that there are no ants or other creatures where you intend to put your hand. This is especially important at night. Most cases of insect stings occur when the organism is inadvertently grabbed or its nest is unknowingly disturbed. Large black ants to be particularly avoided due to their painful sting are the giant hunting ants, known locally as *izula*. They can often be seen foraging on the leaves and branches of shrubs as well as in leaf litter. These shiny ants can grow up to an inch and a half long and have a rather formidable appearance, making it doubtful that anyone would handle them. Problems arise when these ants are unintentionally grabbed, stepped on, or sat upon. Local inhabitants report the sting to be extremely painful and capable of causing a fever that lasts for more than a day. More reliable and less exaggerated reports however compare the effects of their sting to that of a large wasp, painful and unpleasant, but normally not life-threatening. Giant hunting ants tend to make their nests in soil at the base of trees where they can live in colonies of over a hundred individuals. Their venom is sometimes used in the preparation of dart poison.

Due to the mossy nature of the forest at the ACEER and ExplorNapo Lodge, some of the insects have evolved physical adaptations that allow them to better blend in with their environment. One species of katydid for example is a mottled green and yellow with its long, wispy, wavy antennae. Its camouflage is so effective that during the day it sits openly on a moss-covered leaf, relying on its concealing coloration to enable it to go unnoticed. Grasshoppers are also found with a striking moss-like appearance, making them virtually indistinguishable from the carpets of moss they inhabit.

Walkingsticks are among the most cryptic of rainforest invertebrates. Both their coloration and body form permit them to blend in with an environment composed mainly of plant material. Most are wingless, but the males of some can fly and may flutter slowly away when disturbed from their daytime resting place. One of the most spectacular and unusual species is the firestick, which defies normal walkingstick behavior by moving around during the day when it can be seen. Unlike its dull-colored relatives, the firestick has a red-orange head, tail and leg joints. It also has yellow stripes, making it look as if it is

Fig. 8-6   Tarantulas are large, hairy tropical spiders that often live in underground burrows as adults, but may also be found in trees and in roof thatch.

trying to call attention to itself. This may well be the case, as its survival depends on predators recognizing it. If a toucan or monkey has sampled a firestick before and been sickened by it, chances are they will remember and leave it alone the next time they see it.

One organism, sometimes seen on the forest floor, is the tropical flatworm. Stretching at times to a length of more than a foot, these ribbon-like creatures have a glistening, mucus-covered body that is usually a vivid blue and black or yellow and black. Although you may initially mistake it for a colorful leech, it is a scavenger and predator related to the planarians. Terrestrial flatworms belong to a very restricted group and can only live in hot, humid environments such as those found in tropical rainforests.

Night Walks

The forest is a different world at night, at once menacing and foreboding due to restricted visibility and a cacophony of unidentifiable sounds. Although somewhat intimidating to the first-time visitor, a slow walk along a tropical forest trail after dark is an unforgettable experience. Diurnal creatures are at rest, some hidden in nocturnal roosts while others sleep exposed but immobile. Creatures of the night however are active - - in the trees above, on the forest floor below, and on the foliage all around. The best way to see them is by walking slowly and quietly, using a flashlight or headlamp to continually scan the trees and leaves for movement and/or eyeshine. Animals high up in a tree may be difficult to see, but often make their presence known with a thrashing of leaves seemingly out of proportion to their size.

Frogs abound in the humid tropics, and except for the colorful dart-poison frogs, night is the best time to see them. From tiny specimens no bigger than your thumbnail to gargantuan examples that rival the largest of bullfrogs, these photogenic amphibians are out looking for food. It is not uncommon to find one with the legs or antennae of a hapless insect still protruding from its mouth. The laughing frog (genus *Osteocephalus*) is one of the species that develop in bromeliads. The chuckle-like call of the male can often be traced to such plants. The Argentine horned frog (*Ceratophrys cornuta*) is a large, squat, green and black specimen that looks somewhat like a beanbag. It likes to hunker down in the leaf litter with only its head exposed, ambushing prey as it comes by. This bizarre looking amphibian has two large

Fig. 8-7   Piper bushes belong to the pepper family and produce upright fruit stalks fed upon by bats.

Fig. 8-8   A leaf-nosed bat uses sonar and echolocation to locate the insects upon which it feeds.

horns over the eyes and an extremely wide mouth that allows it to take prey consisting of insects, lizards, other frogs, and in some cases even small mammals!

Tree frogs all have a certain "look" about them, regardless of their size, with large protruding eyes and long fingers and toes with sucker-like disks that allow them to stick vertically to tree trunks in classic poses. Almost all are sit-and-wait predators of insects. One particularly unusual looking genus (*Hemiphractus*) found at the ACEER has a large triangular head and broods its eggs on the back of the female. The giant ground frogs (*Leptodactylus* spp.) are among the largest of Amazonian frogs attaining a body length of 4-5 inches. Also known as the "whooping frogs", males will sit in shallow swamps or holes in the ground producing a series of loud whoops that echo throughout the forest. When caught in a flashbeam, the eyes glow like red-hot coals. They are surprisingly agile and difficult to catch for a big frog and can emit a disconcertingly human-like cry when handled.

The jungle paths at night are patrolled by bats which may swoop silently to within inches of your face, with only the flap and breeze of their wings betraying their passage. Foliage-gleaning bats hang from perches, listening intently for sounds of insect origin that could signal their next meal. Piles of moth and katydid wings beneath their perches are testaments to their past successes. When the movement of an insect is detected, the bat leaves its perch and deftly picks off the arthropod from leaf or branch, then returns to its perch where it will hang upside down and eat it.

Leaf-nosed bats (Family Phyllostomidae) are represented by over a hundred neotropical species. They are so called for the leaf-like flap that protrudes above their nose and serves to focus the echolocation sounds emitted to locate prey. Vampire bats also occur in the Amazon, but pose little threat to humans, most often concentrating on horses or cattle as their source of blood. Bats are important both in the regeneration of tropical forests and in the pollination of many jungle trees and plants. Bat-pollinated species produce large, open, night-blooming flowers that use distinctive odors to serve as attractants and locators. The angel's trumpet (*Datura* spp.) with its large hanging, bell-like blossom is a good example.

If you are fortunate, your night hike may allow you to see a snake. Perhaps the most common non-venomous species is the slender snail-eater (Genus *Inmatodes*). Although it grows 3-4 feet long, the body is seldom thicker than a pencil. This serpent has brown and white bands and a small round head. Amazingly, it can stretch almost its entire body length without any support. It poses no threat to humans and is often found in vegetation 6-10 feet above the ground.

Nighttime is also the realm of the spider, and a flashlight shined in almost any direction is sure to catch the reflection from the eyes of several. The eyeshine seen from nocturnally active animals is the light bouncing back off a structure in their eye called the tapetum. By reflecting ambient light outwards, a second opportunity is given to strike the light-sensitive pigments that result in motion detection and image formation. This adaptation is seen in species as widely separated as predatory cats to sphinx moths.

The most impressive spider is the tarantula with its large size, furry body, and huge fangs. Some species use their body hairs as a defense, kicking them off the abdomen and into the eyes of an attacker. Although tarantulas may be seen amongst the foliage and are occasionally spotted in the roof thatch of the buildings, the majority dig burrows in the ground. Their subterranean lair is often excavated surprisingly deep, and you have to be quick while walking to catch more than just a glimpse of a hairy leg as the spider darts back down into its hole.

Two other spider groups, each with its own tactics and strategy for prey capture, are the orb weavers and the ogre-face spiders. Orb weaver is a generic term applied to those species that spin the large, generally rounded webs which ensnare insects. Some of the larger webs are begun only after dark and taken in again before daylight, although some species like the golden silk spider (*Nephila clavipes*) leave their silken nets out all day long. Ogre-face spiders also spin webs, but much smaller ones that they hold in the claws of their front four legs. Firmly attached to a twig or a branch by their rear four legs, they push their small rectangular webs onto unsuspecting insects as they pass within reach. Entangled in the sticky, silken bonds, the arthropods are easy prey.

A group of nocturnal insects that can be found in the forest at any of the lodge sites is the katydids (Family Tettigoniidae). Also known as bush crickets or longhorned grasshoppers, most have extremely long antennae that are covered with sensory receptors used to examine the environment. As with other groups of animals, the number of tropical species and their diversity far exceeds those found in temperate

Fig. 8-10   Tree frogs all have sucker-like disks on their toes.

Fig. 8-9   The famed "whooping frog", which is most often heard before it rains.

Fig. 8-11   A dendrobatid or dart-poison frog.

Fig. 8-12   The Argentine horned frog is also known as a wide-mouthed frog. It is well camouflaged among the leaf litter of the forest floor.

regions. The country of Peru alone has more than 600 species of katydids, at least 80 of which are newly described from field locations near Explorama's lodges and reserves.

Katydids are for the most part gentle, foliage-feeding insects that spend the day hidden or motionless in an attempt to avoid being eaten by sharp-eyed birds, monkeys, and a host of other predators. It is only after dark that they exit the safety of their diurnal resting places to search for food. The wonderful diversity of form and color that they exhibit is at its highest in the tropical forest. Among the most spectacular of all katydids are the leaf-mimicking species.

There are over a hundred described species of true leaf-mimicking katydids that have been collected from the rainforests of South and Central America. Their disguises go far beyond a general resemblance to foliage afforded to most katydids with oval, green wings. Indeed, millions of years of evolution have led to visual adaptations that are both startling and incredible. It seems that for every type of leaf that exists in the forest, an insect counterpart exists among the katydids. There are different colors, shapes, and sizes, sometimes even within the same species between male and female. One specimen may be lush green in color with wings that terminate in an imitation drip-tip and legs and antennae that resemble twigs. Another may be totally brown, with large notches in the wings to give it a chewed, torn, or worn appearance. Others have moldy spots and fake decay areas, convincing indications of a leaf that has begun to rot in the humid tropical environment.

Things are seldom what they seem in the jungle. The peacock katydids are the largest and most spectacular of the leaf mimics. Their primary defense is superlative camouflage as dead, diseased, or decaying leaves. When disturbed however, an unexpected secondary defense comes into play. The peacock katydid orients the rear of its body to the disturbance while simultaneously snapping its wings open. The normally concealed hindwings and undersurface of the forewings are pigmented with vivid orange and purple, as well as an eyespot. The overall effect is one of initial surprise followed by intimidation, caused by what appears to be a face to face confrontation with a much larger animal than expected. After displaying for a short period, the insect hops or flutters away, closing its wings and disappearing again among the leaf litter of the forest floor.

There are numerous other katydids you may see on your night hikes. The spiny lobster is the largest. This big, brown, five-inch long short-winged katydid looks more like a child's wind-up toy than a living creature. The rainbow katydid is the most colorful and aptly named, for it has a blue and yellow abdomen with the legs and rest of the body pigmented with orange, white, green, and blue. One of the few neotropical katydids to have evolved warning coloration, rainbow katydids arch their abdomen and release a warning odor when they are bothered. Field experiments have shown them to be distasteful to large predators such as monkeys. The impaler katydid is one of the few predaceous species. Long, dagger-like spines on the front legs used for capturing and holding prey are responsible for its name.

Perhaps the king of the katydids for making an impression is the spiny devil. This member of the katydid subfamily known as "coneheads" is large, fearsome, and bizarre. Its head is ringed with a margin of big yellow spines with a huge red horn protruding from the top. The legs are also spine-covered, making it difficult for any predator to grab or eat this species. If molested, the front legs are held wide and the mandibles open up in a very effective threatening posture. While most katydids are harmless gentle creatures, this is one of the few that can inflict a painful bite and draw blood.

As you walk along the trails or lie in your bed at night you may hear the "hoo-hoo-hoo-hoo" of the spectacled owl. Its call brings to mind the name of "hoot owl". It is a large owl at 18", and feeds on a variety of animals and insects of all kinds. Spectacled owls can sometimes be attracted or "called in" by imitating their calls.

Not far down the trail from the ACEER facilities you can experience an unusual phenomenon. It must be at night and requires shutting off your flashlight. As your eyes slowly adapt to the darkness, you will become aware that there is a strange luminescence all around you. This is actually a luminescent fungus growing in the leaf litter. The fungus is difficult to discern with the naked eye and it is often disappointing to turn your flashlight back on and see no outward sign of anything unusual where it occurs.

Fig. 8-13   With its wings closed, the peacock katydid looks like a diseased leaf.

Fig. 8-14   *The peacock katydid above is in full intimidation display. When disturbed, this large katydid snaps open its wings to reveal bright colors and eyespots. A predator may be startled and remain confused long enough for the katydid to hop or flutter away, close its wings, and blend in with the other leaves of the forest.*

Fig. 8-15   The Amazon Canopy Walkway is the largest of its kind in the world. Its suspended spans zig-zag from one emergent support tree to the next, extending for a quarter of a mile through the treetops.

The Amazon Canopy Walkway

The most unique attraction of ExplorNapo, ExplorTambos and the ACEER field station is access to the Canopy Walkway. CONAPAC and the ACEER Foundation are joint owners of the walkway, with CONAPAC responsible for its daily maintenance. The concept of the Canopy Walkway came about as the result of the First International Rainforest Workshop conducted at Explorama's lodges in 1991. Expertise from engineers, tropical biologists, and people in the tourism and travel industries was carefully considered before beginning construction.

Many individuals played major roles in bringing the Canopy Walkway from an idea to reality. Peter Jenson of Explorama Tours and Richard Ryel of International Expeditions were responsible for funding the project in its initial stages. Dr. Illar Muul, having overseen the design and construction of several canopy walkways in Malaysia and China, was essential for planning the route and design for the walkway. Paul Donahue and Teresa Wood, an American couple with vast tropical experience, worked at the site for several years during the walkway's construction. Their desire to observe canopy-inhabiting bird species led them to master the climbing techniques necessary for canopy access. The skills for ascending into the upper levels of the forest, which they taught to the local Peruvian team, were put to the test as they participated in the walkway construction while suspended from ropes on a daily basis.

The Peruvian team was and is led by master carpenter Don Victor Sevillano. An employee of Explorama since its creation 35 years ago, Don Victor can take credit for directing the construction of all the buildings at each of Explorama's facilities as well as designing the unique structure of each of the Canopy Walkway platforms. The Canopy Walkway definitely proved to be his greatest challenge. Many others took an active part in the climbing and building of the Canopy Walkway including Teddy Padilla and Victor Inuacari who are still a part of the maintenance team.

The Canopy Walkway site was selected after surveying and analyzing the topography of the area. A tract of land encompassing a ridge top and numerous emergent trees was chosen. By utilizing this existing ridge, additional altitude was gained resulting in spectacular vistas from the tallest platforms. Delivery of essential components for the walkway was a logistical nightmare. Items were shipped to Peru from all

Fig. 8-16   Bromeliads and other epiphytic plants flourish in the upper levels of the rainforest.

Fig. 8-17   Bromeliads sometimes occur in dense clusters. The fortunate visitor may see them while in bloom.

Fig. 8-18   A huge philodendron spreads its large triangular leaves eighty feet above the ground.

Fig. 8-19   *The morning sun illuminates one of the spans on the Canopy Walkway. Quiet observers are treated to a myriad of bird species engaging in their daily activities in the boughs of the surrounding trees.*

Fig. 8-20   Don Victor Sevillano is the master carpenter who designed the Canopy Walkway platforms and who has supervised the construction of all of Explorama's lodges.

Fig. 8-21   Paul Donahue and Teresa Wood supervised, trained, and led the climbing teams who did the upper level construction work of the walkway.

Fig. 8-22   Teddy Padilla participated as a climbing crew member throughout the building of the Canopy Walkway and continues as part of the maintenance team.

Fig. 8-23   Don Antonio Montero Pisco, a man of many talents, learned climbing skills and contributed his efforts to the walkway construction as well.

over the world, including the original ladders which came from Malaysia. Upon arrival in Iquitos, the necessary tools and construction materials had to then be sent downriver to the Canopy Walkway site.

Work on the walkway began in September of 1991. The Canopy Walkway first opened to visitors while only partially completed in June of 1992. It took another year to finish the project and by the end of 1993, the walkway was complete. It is almost 1,200 feet long, stretching through the treetops for a distance of almost a quarter of a mile. In total, the walkway is composed of spans that are suspended between 14 giant support trees. It is the longest structure of its kind in the world. At its highest point, it towers 120 feet above the ground and affords an unprecedented view of the forest. The Canopy Walkway is actually a series of suspended or hanging bridges that zig-zag from one large support tree to another. There are entrance and exit towers which are not high in themselves, but serve as access points to enter and leave, eliminating the need to double back.

The main support for each span or bridge are large wire cables. Polyester ropes spaced periodically along these cables are suspended vertically and threaded through sections of the special metal ladders that are laid flat, parallel to the plane of the ground. Wooden planks, fastened in place on top of the rungs of the ladders, provide a stable, if somewhat narrow, boardwalk. The sides of each span are formed by a wide nylon mesh woven taut between the support ropes. Thousands of people have now traversed the Canopy Walkway with no greater mishap than dropping a lens cap or forgetting a roll of film.

As you walk out on the first span, it bounces slightly and sways with your step. After a few paces you can stop though, and just enjoy the view which only gets better and better. The upper levels of the forest and canopy are strata that are usually viewed from below or by airplane from above. It is unique to be within the canopy itself, observing the bromeliads, orchids, beaver-tail lizards, and ants that live out their daily lives a hundred or so feet above the forest floor.

The first span ends at a platform that is built around the entire trunk of the support tree. A set of stairs lead to another platform just above it. This unique double platform design results in 10-15 feet of additional height at each support tree. This design, the natural incline of each successive span, and the location along a natural ridge takes the walkway to increasingly higher elevations. The highest point,

Fig. 8-24   Individual walkway spans zig-zag their way through the canopy.

Fig. 8-25   Each walkway span connects to a platform with one to three levels which provide additional height. These platforms provide an ideal place for birdwatching.

Fig. 8-26   *Sunrise and sunset are times of great tranquility from the lofty perches of the Canopy Walkway. Above is a late afternoon vista as seen from one of the support platforms.*

approximately 120 feet above the ground, is reached at Platform #6. A favorite spot for early-morning birders, Platform #6 provides the uncommon opportunity to watch canopy birds at their level as they join to form mixed flocks for the day. The Canopy Walkway is especially impressive in the solitude that precedes sunrise and sunset. Whatever the time or one's reason for visiting, the Canopy Walkway remains an unforgettable experience.

Platform #6 has another attraction, but it is herpetological rather than avian in nature. Hard to miss for anyone who spends more that a few minutes on this platform during the day is the resident troop of lizards that occupy the tree. They are the famed Amazon thorny-tails (*Tropidurus flaviceps*), although they may also be called beaver-tail or shovel-tail lizards. These fearless arboreal lizards have a large, flat, spiny tail which accounts for their variety of common names. The males are larger (up to about 8") and have an orange or reddish head. The smaller females tend to have bright yellow heads. These lizards are comical to watch as they gobble up ants that walk by them on the tree. Sometimes they don't even change position, merely lunging their head forward to pick off the ants one after the other. Unwary tourists should not be startled if one of these lizards climbs up a pant leg or hops on an arm for a closer look.

Fig. 8-27   The Amazon thorny-tail lizard, a commonly seen canopy inhabitant.

Most visitors find it difficult to leave the Canopy Walkway, so enchanting are the vistas and opportunities for bird watching. Yet all good things must come to an end, and once you have walked the last span you find yourself at an exit tower that provides steps and easy access to the forest floor. The trail back to ExplorNapo or the ACEER begins immediately at the base of the tower.

Summary

As with most things in life, a trip to the rainforest is what you make of it. People travel for different reasons and with different goals in mind. The objective of a biologist may differ from that of a tourist or film crew or photographer. However, whatever your goal, the tropical forest surrounding Explorama's lodges and reserves is without a doubt one of the areas of greatest biological diversity on the face of the Earth. It provides an unprecedented opportunity for research, study, and education in formal course-oriented situations, as well as a delightful chance for hikers and naturalists to just enjoy observing nature.

Explorama has spent over 35 years developing the most comfortable and visitor-friendly accommodations in the Amazon. Efficient logistical support, meticulously organized facilities, well mantained trail systems, excellent cuisine, knowledgeable multi-lingual guides, and a friendly staff of long-time employees permit visitors to concentrate on one thing - - enjoying their trip. Given today's logistical capabilities, there is no longer a reason for anyone not to explore the great and wonderful Amazon Rainforest!

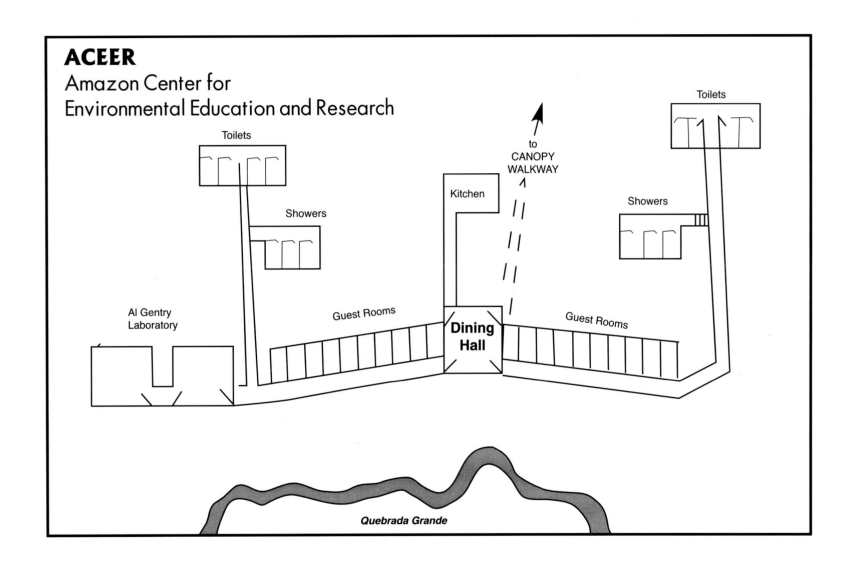

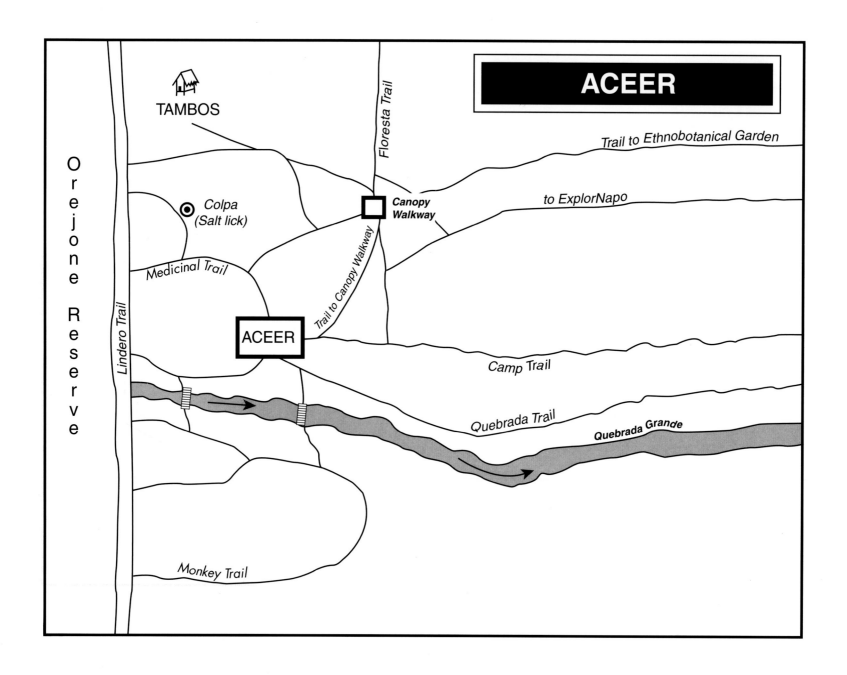

ACEER

TAMBOS

Floresta Trail

Trail to Ethnobotanical Garden

to ExplorNapo

Colpa
(Salt lick)

Canopy
Walkway

Orejone Reserve

Medicinal Trail

Trail to Canopy Walkway

Lindero Trail

ACEER

Camp Trail

Quebrada Trail

Quebrada Grande

Monkey Trail

References and Resources

This section is provided for those interested in obtaining more information about the rainforest. There are thousands of titles that deal with various aspects of tropical forests and although it would be impossible to list them all, five or six books have been placed under each specific subheading that follows. A much more comprehensive listing of books dealing with the rainforest is provided at the Rainforest Information Center website. Most titles have an accompanying description and can be ordered directly from the bookstore at this site. The address is:

Rainforest Information Center
www.rainforestinfo.com

Books

Historical and Exploration

The Naturalist On The Rivers Amazon, Henry Bates, 1910.
Through The Brazilian Wilderness, Theodore Roosevelt, 1969 (first published in 1914).
A Narrative Of Travels On The Amazon And Rio Negro, Alfred Wallace, 1889.
The Putumayo - The Devil's Paradise, W. Hardenburg, 1912.
Notes Of A Botanist On The Amazon And Andes, Richard Spruce, 1908.
Explorers Of The Amazon, Anthony Smith, 1990.

Coffee Table Books

Amazonia, Loren McIntyre, 1991.
Portraits Of The Rainforest, Adrian Forsyth, 1990.
The Rainforests - A Celebration, Lisa Silcock (editor), 1989.
Rainforests, Norman Myers, 1993.
The Rainforest, D 'Arcy Richardson, 1991.

General

Tropical Nature, Adrian Forsyth and Ken Miyata, 1987.
A Neotropical Companion, John Kricher, 1989.
Floods Of Fortune, Michael Goulding, Nigel Smith, and Dennis Mahar, 1996.
Tropical Rainforest, Arnold Newman, 1990.
In The Rainforest, Catherine Caufield, 1984.

Adventure

La Doctora, Linnea Smith, 1999.
A Parrot Without A Name, Don Stap, 1990.
One River, Wade Davis, 1996.
White Waters And Black, Gordon MacGreagh, 1926 (republished in 1985).
Brazilian Adventure, Peter Fleming, 1960.

Medicinal Plants and Ethnobotany

A Field Guide To Medicinal And Useful Plants Of The Upper Amazon, James Castner, Stephen Timme and James Duke, 1998.
Amazonian Ethnobotanical Dictionary, James Duke and Rodolfo Vasquez, 1994.

Medicinal Plants and Ethnobotany (continued)

Wizard Of The Upper Amazon, Bruce Lamb, 1974.
The Healing Forest, Richard Schultes and Robert Raffauf, 1990.
Tales Of A Shaman's Apprentice, Mark Plotkin, 1993.

Rainforest Canopy and Biodiversity

Life Above The Jungle Floor, Donald Perry, 1986.
High Frontier, Mark Moffett, 1994.
The Enchanted Canopy, Andrew Mitchell, 1986.
Biodiversity, Edward Wilson (editor), 1988.
Life In The Treetops, Margaret Lowman, 1999.

Flora and Fauna Guides

Amazon Insects - A Photo Guide, James Castner, 2000.
A Guide To The Birds Of Colombia, Steven Hilty and Wiliam Brown, 1986.
Neotropical Rainforest Mammals, Louise Emmons, 1990.
Guide To The Frogs Of The Iquitos Region, Amazonian Peru, Lily Rodriguez and William Duellman, 1994
Butterflies Of South America, Bernard D'Abrera, 1984.

Books for Biologists

Four Neotropical Rainforests, Alwyn Gentry (editor), 1990.
La Selva, Lucinda McDade and others (editors), 1994.
The Ecology Of A Tropical Forest, Egbert Leigh, Jr. and others (editors), 1982.
Costa Rican Natural History, Daniel Janzen (editor), 1983.
Tropical Rainforests, Frank Almeda and Catherine Pringle (editors), 1988.

Books for Teachers

The Amazon Rainforest - An Exploration Of Countries, Cultures And Creatures - A Learning Center For Secondary School Students, James Castner, 1999.
A Unit About Tropical Rainforests, Debby DePauw, 1993.
Using The Internet To Explore Rain Forests, Jan Nutt, 1997.
South America - A Homework Booklet, Harriet Kinghorn, Helen Colella and Diane Fusaro, 1996.

Books for Children

Deep In The Amazon, James Castner, 2001.
Bats, Bugs, And Biodiversity, Susan Goodman and Michael Doolittle, 1995.
Go And Come Back, Joan Abelove, 1998.
A Walk In The Rainforest, Kristin Pratt, 1992. (Available in Spanish)
Living Treasure, Laurence Pringle, 1991.

Art and Artifacts

Arts Of The Amazon, Barbara Braun (editor), 1995.
Arts And Crafts Of South America, Lucie Davies and Mo Finey, 1994.
The Gift Of Birds, Ruben Reina and Kenneth Kensinger (editors), 1991.
Crafts Of Ecuador, Pablo Cuvi, 1994.
Indian Art In South America, Frederick Dockstader, 1967.

Indigenous Peoples and Tribes

People Of The Tropical Rain Forest, Julie Denslow and Christine Padoch (editors), 1988.
Makuna - Portrait Of An Amazonian People, Kaj Århem, 1998.
The Jívaro - People Of The Sacred Waterfalls, Michael Harner, 1972.

About The Author

Dr. Jim Castner is a tropical biologist-photographer-writer who has traveled throughout South and Central America during the past twenty years. He has worked as a Scientific Photographer for a major university and is currently an Adjunct Professor in the Biology Department at Pittsburg State University in Pittsburg, Kansas. He has conducted research on the insect fauna of the Explorama reserves and the ACEER for over a decade with support in the form of field volunteer assistants from Earthwatch. During this time he has made over 50 trips to the Explorama Lodges and Peru.

Dr. Castner's photographs have appeared in a variety of books and magazines, including almost every college-level biology textbook. His favorite topics are related to the rainforest and the insect world. Some of his writing and photo credits include: *National Geographic, Natural History, International Wildlife, GEO, GeoMundo, National Geographic World, Ranger Rick,* and *Kids Discover*. His book credits include: *1) Amazon Insects - A Photo Guide, 2) A Field Guide To Medicinal And Useful Plants Of The Upper Amazon, 3) The Amazon Rainforest - An Exploration of Countries, Cultures, and Creatures, 4) Forensic Entomology,* and *5) Photographic Guide To Forensic Insects*. Dr. Castner is currently working on a series of children's books on the flora, fauna, and people of the rainforest to be published by Marshall Cavendish and tentatively titled *Deep In The Amazon*.

In 1997, Dr. Castner left his academic position to pursue writing and the development of educational materials full-time. He has been actively involved as an educator of secondary school students for many years, often acting as a workshop leader or instructor of field courses. He designs and leads natural history tours for teachers, students, and naturalists to the Amazon Basin with the company Rainforest Ventures. He often serves as a consultant in many capacities. Dr. Castner is the creator of the **Information Center Web Ring** whose web sites may be accessed through: **www.rainforestinfo.com** or at **www.biologicalphotography.com**.

Visiting The Amazon

Many people are intimidated at the thought of visiting the Amazon themselves. However, there are a wide variety of options available for people of all ages and physical conditions. Explorama Tours provides facilities that range from air-conditioned luxury in a five star hotel to the primitive experience of camping out in the jungle. Their jungle lodges have hosted commercial tour groups, educational workshops and classes, as well as individual visitors for over 35 years. To contact them directly, please look at the information below:

EXPLORAMA LODGES
Box 446
Iquitos, PERU

Phone: (51-94) 25-3301
(51-94) 25-2526
Fax: (51-94) 25-2533

E-Mail: amazon@explorama.com
Web Site: http://www.explorama.com

USA / CANADA Reservations (SACA): Phone 1 -800-707-5275